Available formats: E-book, hardcover, paperback, and audiobook.
Audio recordings for guided practices are available at www.fierceboundaries.com.
Cover created using Canva Pro. Image by Darya Fedorova.

Resources for survivors of relational violence: www.safewithinwellness.com

All graphics and cover designed by Cynthia Garner

Paperback ISBN 979-8-9904151-1-9

Safe Within
Publications

FIERCE BOUNDARIES

*Practical Skills and Somatic Exercises for
Healing in a Traumatized World*

CYNTHIA GARNER

Safe Within Publications
Boulder, CO.

For Hazel and Debra, with a deep bow of gratitude and respect.
Thank you for having the courage to be
a light in the darkness.

Table of Contents

Guided Mindfulness and Somatic Exercises

Downloadable audio recordings are available at fierceboundaries.com.

1.1: Fist Experiment – 3 minutes

1.2: Introductory Mindfulness Practice – 12 minutes

2.1: S.T.O.P (poster)/Press Pause – 3 minutes

3.1: Awareness of Breath – 9 minutes

3.2: Awareness of Physical Sensations – 9 minutes

3.3: Awareness of Seeing – 5 minutes

3.4: Awareness of Sound with Bells – 6 minutes

3.5: Object Meditation – 6 minutes

4.1: Resourcing Practice – 13 minutes

5.2: Gratitude Practice – 14 minutes

5.3: Savoring Practice – 9 minutes

6.3: Gratitude Body Scan – 20 minutes

6.4: MBSR Body Scan – 35 minutes

6.5: Standing Body Scan – 5 minutes

6.6: Standing Body Scan with Movement – 20 minutes

7.1: Awareness of Difficult Sensations – 9 minutes

7.2: Gentle Mindful Movement (video) – 15 minutes

9.1: Loving Kindness for Yourself – 9 minutes

9.2: Soften, Soothe, Allow – 9 minutes

10.2: Awareness of Thoughts – 13 minutes

12.1: Loving Kindness for Others – 14 minutes

I alone cannot change the world,
but I can cast a stone across the waters to create many ripples.
-Mother Theresa

Prologue: The Plight of the People-Pleaser

Before I finally blocked communication with my ex-husband, eight years after our divorce, he texted and emailed me multiple times a day blaming me for his unhappiness and anger. I don't blame him, because I've enabled his abuse since the day we met, when I decided it was my job to save him from himself. I could see his potential behind those dark, brooding eyes and forced smile, and when he rejected my advances, claiming he was too broken for love, I felt the thrill of the chase. Challenge accepted.

I am a people-pleaser through and through and I've always been the one who is good at taking care of everyone else's needs and doing the saving. Since I was a young child and my parents adopted two siblings from El Salvador, I've been the one who no one needed to worry about, who had it all together, and who played the role of peacemaker in the family. I could see how much my brother and sister struggled to adjust, and I worked hard to make sure my parents could count on me to do well in school, not take up too much space, and manage my own emotions, without help. They already had enough on their plates with two scarred and traumatized children. By not having needs of my own and doing everything myself, I got to take care of them, too.

My core beliefs about how the world worked were built around being of service to others and setting myself aside for the "greater good." I suppose that since I was raised without an understanding of how to put my own wellbeing before those who were suffering, it makes sense that I married a depressed alcoholic and became an over-extended, underpaid schoolteacher. But, after seven years of pouring my heart out for my students and my disastrous marriage, my well finally ran dry and my spirit broke. It's true what they say – *if you do not tend to your wellness, you'll be forced to tend to your illness.*

The year we divorced was the worst of my adult life, and in addition to the devastating grief of losing the large family I'd always dreamed of having, I faced an endless barrage of severe logistical, physical, and mental health challenges. My ex-husband couldn't manage himself well enough to be a reliable source of care or pay child support, and he was often emotionally abusive and suicidal. Because he blamed me and our divorce for his predicament, he texted me accusations and threats of self-harm throughout my workday. I regularly experienced panic attacks and such severe muscle spasms that I had trouble performing the basic functions of my job.

During what would end up being my final semester in the classroom, I developed severe anxiety, lost part of my hearing due to a prolonged sinus infection, and struggled to make ends meet financially as a single mother. I also ruptured a disc in my lower back putting me in a wheelchair and preventing me from being able to lift a bag of groceries, much less my three-year-old daughter. Years of disregarding my own emotional, mental, and physical health, the stress of the job, the weight of abuse, and my overwhelm had broken me.

Over the summer, I recovered from a successful micro-discectomy and slowly regained mobility in my leg. During this process, I enrolled in a Mindfulness-Based Stress Reduction course (MBSR), an eight-week, evidence-based program that offers secular mindfulness training to help people with chronic pain, stress, anxiety, and depression. The body awareness practices, gentle yoga, and cognitive exercises had a profound impact on me and for the first time in many years, I started to believe that healing was possible. As soon as I completed the MBSR course, I signed up for professional training so that I could teach it to others and went back to school to also learn counseling and somatic psychotherapy.

There was finally light on the horizon. By carving out time for these longer periods of body awareness and mindfulness meditation, and with a clearer understanding of how my choices affected my nervous system and attentional control, my body, mind, and heart began to recover. I learned that setting boundaries that honored my needs improved my wellbeing and that befriending my experience helped me be less reactive. One breath at a time I developed the capacity to reclaim my attention, and to notice the triggers, habits, and automatic thoughts that kept me stuck in relational turmoil.

However, the more tools I put in my toolkit, the more the world tested me. Growing my capacity to tolerate discomfort and cope skillfully seemed to attract larger waves of emotional upheaval and more drama into my life. My practice helped, but it didn't stop my ex from harassing me. Just when I thought I was getting somewhere, I'd get another flurry of text messages, he'd sink into another episode, my body would contract with muscle spasms and anxiety, and my mind would race with intrusive thoughts. The cycle was endless and exhausting.

When I was triggered, which was often, meditation was especially difficult. Sitting down and trying to be still in a state of heightened anxiety had the opposite effect. At first, I felt the initial rush of relief from adopting the familiar posture of paying attention. But, as I tried to sustain attention with the sensations of breathing, I was bombarded with images of violence, overtaken by inexplicable rage and grief, and paralyzed with terror. Within a few minutes of sitting to meditate, desperate for a moment of relief, I'd pop off the cushion in a panic. I couldn't escape the feelings of constant anxiety and felt like silent meditation practice was yet another thing I had failed to master. *Meditation doesn't work for me*, I thought. *It only makes things worse.*

For a long time, I coped by drinking and smoking pot, because tuning out and numbing to the world seemed like the only way to escape the torment of my mind. Eventually, however, my therapist and my counseling training offered me language and tools to understand that my attachment trauma and the experience of witnessing violence before my adoption as a baby were stored in my body's cellular memory. The stories of abuse and abandonment lived in my bones and were still playing out in my relationships, addictions, and daily life.

Using many of the tools I have laid out for you in the following chapters, I was finally able to access and alchemize this undischarged traumatic energy and to stop letting it control me. Simple trauma-sensitive changes, such as taking agency, opening my eyes, naming my feelings, honoring my body, and allowing myself some movement during meditation, meetings, and conversations with my ex, made all the difference in my personal practice. Setting boundaries internally for myself and prioritizing my own mental health helped me stop losing myself to fear and reactivity, which turned out to be much more important than building impenetrable walls that would keep the danger out.

My therapeutic skills and mindfulness practice were put to the test with the global pandemic. During this time of social distancing, extreme stress, and worst-case scenarios, many of my timid new boundaries were compromised and eventually collapsed. I endured yet another prolonged period of harassment and emotional abuse from my ex-husband, primarily through digital communication.

No matter how many times I demanded he stop, the hateful messages from him kept coming, even in response to simple logistical questions like "can you pick up our daughter from school?" In his responses, he threatened to leave the country, or to hurt himself, and claimed that his life was worthless and that it was all my fault. They were the same conversations we had always had, and though it had been eight years since our divorce, things weren't getting any easier. His constant harassment and the way he jabbed at my abandonment wounds and compromised the healing I had worked so hard for in therapy were a constant invasion of my right to peace. His accusations, threats, and attacks invaded my thoughts and kept me awake at night. I became short-tempered with my daughter, which broke my heart, because all I've ever wanted was to be the mom I didn't get to have.

One day, after another round of accusations that I was the one manipulating and abusing him, I felt the need to prove to myself that I wasn't crazy. So, I printed out all the threatening emails and screenshots of the text messages I'd saved over the years as "evidence" and matched them up with the "warning signs of emotional abuse" I had recently added to my website. One of the symptoms of emotional abuse is feeling like you're the one to blame for the conflict and doubting your own experience. **"Gaslighting"** is a subtle tactic of manipulation in which your feelings are invalidated, and you start to believe that the abuse is your fault and that you are the one with the problem.

My ex's behavior was exactly this — he couldn't pay his rent, couldn't find work that didn't break his body, and when I gave him money to help, he responded by telling me that sacrificing his life to stay here and be a father was a "death sentence." He called me "your majesty," and a "control freak." My phone and email inbox pulsed endlessly with threats, blame, desperation, pleas for money, and so many reminders of why we divorced in the first place. By shifting blame back to me, he avoided responsibility. By making me question my reality, he kept me locked in the cycle of defensiveness and co-dependency. If he could make me feel as scared and alone as he was, only then would he feel "understood." So he kept me trapped as his scapegoat, so that he could feed off me, because he was a vampire and I had been his energy source since the day we met.

I knew he was not well and had finally recognized it wasn't possible for me to make him better. I also knew that blaming him or keeping our daughter away from him were not good solutions and doing so would only result in more conflict. And even though my therapist told me that his recent behaviors lined up with the diagnosis for narcissistic personality disorder, and that his accusations were symptoms of his illness, just like sneezes are a symptom of a cold, I still got caught up in his psychosis.

I was still the great villain in his life story, just as he was the great villain in mine. He lived his life in victim mode, which is the worst because it spirals on itself, just like depression, getting worse and worse the more you focus on it. The more I tried to make him feel better, the more he blamed me for his despair. We were trapped in an endless cycle of enabling and abuse. He was fixated on me as the source of his pain and wanted me to suffer as much as he had, and I was just desperate to break free and to be left in peace, but I couldn't seem to stop replying to his messages and trying to help him be a better father. Even though resources about the "narcissist-empath dynamic" told me to stop participating in the dialogue, that replying to him was like "throwing rocks at birds," and that "no response *is* a response," I kept checking my email and eventually writing back, because more than anything, I wanted to help him be well enough to stay in our daughter's life. She needed her dad.

"You don't have to keep funding it," a wise friend told me one morning, as I complained to her about this latest downward spiral over tea. "You need to get fierce with your boundaries."

Dang it, I knew she was right. And I had tried setting boundaries, really, I had. Every morning, I sat for thirty minutes in meditation, and practiced focusing my attention on anchors in the present moment, so I could avoid getting hijacked by intrusive thoughts and keep him from occupying so much of my mental real estate. I had learned to keep his text messages set to "do not disturb," and to filter his emails into a "smart" inbox, so that I couldn't see them on my phone. But knowing there were hateful messages in that hidden folder waiting for me was like a radio playing on the other side of the fence. It penetrated the silence, and destroyed any rest or real peace I could ever hope for.

Plus, how could I set boundaries when our daughter's birthday was coming up, and we had to figure out who was making the cake, and where she was going to spend the night, and which parent was going to host the next sleepover? How could I set boundaries and be *kind* at the same time, when I wanted so badly to help but nothing I did was ever enough? What did *compassion* look like, when what I *really* wanted to do was to file for termination of his parental rights and tell him to please just fucking get lost and never come back, and that we'd all be better off without him?

At home, later that afternoon, the printed stack of "evidence" yelled at me from the pile on my desk. So, I whimsically threw the papers into a metal bucket and lit it on fire. I took it outside and placed it in the yard where the smoke billowed around the house, symbolically cleansing us all from the memory of this toxicity. I got out a giant canvas and a *lot* of paint and I sliced the surface in half with painter's tape, and I let myself have my feelings all over the damn place. The top part of the canvas was where I let my light shine, painting my brilliance with handprints and iridescent, glowing colors. On the bottom of the canvas, I splashed and splattered hues of darkness and fire and smeared them around angrily with a gigantic brush and dramatic, pounding strokes.

Once the pages in the bucket outside burned down to dust, I mixed the ashes with acrylic gesso so that they turned goopy and gray, and added them to the painting, right along the "boundary" between the two sides. Then I pulled up the tape, and laid the canvas down on its back, and ran drippy blood red along the seam between the two very different parts. Then I tipped the painting back up and let the blood run down into the murky, ugly, bottom half, away from the flower garden of my soul and the bright explosion of color that represented my heart.

The next morning, I blocked his number for good and shot him one last email explaining that he could no longer contact me at all. I told him that at ten years old, our daughter was mature enough to decide for herself whether she wanted to spend time with him, and I would no longer be involved. I'd decided to get her a phone so that *she* could be the one to communicate with both of us about what *she* needed. She was old enough and wise enough to be trusted, and I was ready to set her free to have her own experience with her father, even if he was unstable. Because I believed in her capacity to discern the truth for herself, the discomfort of this big leap of faith in her was completely manageable, especially compared to the discomfort of what had been happening for the last eight years. No more.

The next morning, I awoke feeling more refreshed and light-hearted than I had in years, knowing there would be nothing hostile waiting for me on my phone or in my email. The painting, still drying in the living room, was ugly and unsettling, but it made me feel powerful to know that I had set a real boundary this time, and that I would keep it. Still, I didn't like the way the ex-husband part took up so much space and overwhelmed the *me* part. The realistic way the blood dripped down through the gash made it feel harsh and unfinished.

There had to be a way to protect my heart without making myself hard and angry like shards of broken glass. I didn't just want safety in isolation, hidden away from the world behind the iron gates of my fierce determination never to be wounded again. I wanted to be soft and receptive to love, willing to connect and be open-hearted without being exposed and vulnerable to attack. So, I decided to trace around the blood lines in gold, like the Japanese art of *Kintsugi*, where broken pottery is put back together with gold in the cracks.

The idea here is that in embracing flaws and imperfections, it's possible to create an even stronger, more beautiful piece of art. I surrounded all the "blood" with gold and drew trickling lines down into the murky underworld part of the painting, like roots, or lightning, or cracks in the darkness. Satisfied, I called the piece "Resolution," and I hung it over the desk in my writing studio, as a reminder of this commitment to myself.

I would not throw rocks at birds. I would not allow my mental real estate to be occupied by blame and shame, and I would not stoop to the level of hurling accusations back at him, which was like raging at other drivers when I was alone in my car. It was useless, and only hurt me. Stewing in those feelings and that mindset of victimhood was like drinking poison on purpose, and because I was now fully committed to my own wellbeing, I decided to choose peace *all the time*. I choose compassion *all the time*. I choose to place strong protective boundaries around my right to my own happiness and mental health *all the time*, and to do the only thing for him that I could, which was to send kind thoughts to that wounded part of him that learned that he did not belong in the world, from a safe distance, with an open heart.

It had taken me this long to recognize my own role in the ongoing cycle of relational trauma. I had *read* the emails. I had responded to the text messages with my thumbs of fury pounding on my keypad. I was not blaming myself for keeping it going for so long, but I was finally seeing that it truly does take two to tango, and I was responsible for my own part in this mess.

And though I might not be able to stop him from sending the messages or change his mind about his worthiness as a father, I could choose to take responsibility and make my own path forward. I could not control his actions, and after all these years I had finally learned that it was not my job to fix him. Yes, it hurt to recognize that trying to "help" had only magnified his distress and disempowered him to do his own healing. But I didn't want to hurt him anymore because all that hurling abandonment at each other was awful, and I was sick of it. So, I would not participate. I would not check my "smart" email inbox. I would not receive text messages that ungrounded me and spiraled me away from myself, and soon he would have to acknowledge that no response *was* indeed a response, and that he could finally make is own path forward without his resentment of me holding him back.

I would not fund this feud with my blood, time, or tears any longer. I was done.

In the end, getting fierce with my boundaries made all the difference. A few months later, my ex-husband left and moved across the country, leaving my daughter and me on our own, at long last. We parted ways amicably and did not speak until the day he said goodbye. And though it took her some time to navigate the grief and confusion, my daughter has a good-enough long-distance relationship with her father, and I am finally free to stop looking over my shoulder and no longer jump when my phone buzzes. Because I did not engage with him during this transition, and stayed consistent and committed to myself, he had no choice but to stop harassing me.

Despite big feelings, high stress, and bigger life changes, it ended up being one of the most peaceful periods of our relationship, and the beginning of one of the healthiest and happiest times of my life. His departure finally gave me space to forgive and move on. We would always be connected through our daughter, and we could finally love each other in a way that kept both of us safe, by letting each other go.

Some might say that my behavior was selfish. I know my ex-husband certainly would. But ultimately, my boundaries are a matter of survival. With my ex, I still have to be prickly like a cactus, just to protect my right to blossom and continue to grow without being eaten alive. With my daughter I keep my arms wide open, so that she can fall into them whenever she wants to cry. With my own heart I am a fierce guardian with the watchful eye of a night hawk and the attentional control of a lion.

It has not been a particularly easy undertaking to invest in myself so heavily, but it was worth it because now, when I sit on my cushion and close my eyes, I feel peace and joy despite my grief, and I can ride the waves of stress and sadness without getting swept into the sea of panic and despair. I am deeply committed to protecting my right to motherhood, rest, patience, kindness, openness, and presence. These are the qualities my daughter most needs for me to embody so that she can learn to face our traumatized world in her own way, skillfully and knowing that mental health and safe relationships are worth the fight.

On a professional level, I pulled away temporarily from my work with educational leadership and turned my attention fully towards this book. I channeled my fury and love into these pages so that you might have the tools to step into your relationships with a soft, protected heart and a strong "no" in your pocket. My wish for you, dear reader, is that it will help you see that you aren't alone and give you a toolkit that you can carry forward into new relationships and challenges, so that you can be sharp, fierce, and determined to honor yourself when it matters most. Perhaps together we can start a revolution of the heart and guide the next generation into a future with self-care, presence, and wellbeing at the center of our lives.

Introduction: Healing is Possible

The time is here to collectively acknowledge that the grief so many of us are experiencing is real and that we are in a state of collective crisis. We need help, and most of us don't know how to ask for it.

If you are holding this book in your hands, you have already taken a step in the right direction. Asking for help means that you still have a glimmer of hope for the future, and hope makes all the difference. Making this leap is not easy, in fact it is one of the most courageous things you can do. But humans are resilient and strong, and in my personal and professional life I've witnessed that when we bring loving awareness to what is arising, set fierce boundaries around our mental real estate and our relationship to ourselves, and approach suffering with curiosity and care, it results in the mending of hearts that can ripple outward for generations.

I believe that a renaissance in how we tend to ourselves and each other is possible, if we've practiced saying "no" to what does not serve our collective wellbeing, and "yes" to what nourishes us and makes us thrive. The skills and practices I offer within these pages will help you learn to do exactly this, and to welcome you back home to yourself, where you truly belong.

When you are fierce in your boundaries, you don't compromise or let people push at the edges of what makes you who you are. You keep your feet firmly planted beneath you and you dig deep and find that determination, grit, and resolve that it takes to protect your heart, the way a mama bear guards her cubs, the way a tiger stalks her prey. Fierce means honoring your knowing, and knowing you deserve to be treated with exquisite care and regard and settling for nothing less, even from all the past versions of yourself that would have you buckle and give in, still desperate to belong.

Being fierce means refusing to carry the weight of a world in crisis, full of injustice and greed, but listening to the screaming fire in your belly, and instead of shoving it down and letting it turn into anxiety and explosive rage, pushing it up through your throat and speaking your truth out loud, saying *enough! STOP. I deserve better. Our children deserve better. Humanity deserves better. I will not be silent and complacent about my right to own my wellbeing anymore.*

Reckoning with the Task Ahead

Family systems, organizations, schools, and communities across the country are still recovering from the impact of the global pandemic, and many of us are experiencing ever-increasing levels of depression, addiction, chronic stress, mental illness, and interpersonal violence. So many of us are also parents who are navigating not only our own anxiety and overwhelm, but we are also doing what we can to raise children who can cope with the tremendous pressures and threats of our modern world.

Unfortunately, the majority of us in this position were not taught how to effectively manage our own stress, and we were also encouraged to repress our emotions and to numb ourselves with distractions, alcohol, social media, and medication. As a result, we are unequipped to care for ourselves in the face of widespread distress and the fear-based mindset proliferated by the media. We are even less prepared to cope skillfully in the face of the collective trauma of an entire culture that is buckling under the weight of systemic collapse. To heal at the whole-systems level, we must change the story we are telling ourselves.

This book provides a field-tested pathway for this transformation and a new narrative for those of us willing to try a different approach — **prioritizing our own wellbeing and believing that healing is possible**. As the mother of an elementary-aged daughter, a former classroom teacher, a trauma survivor, and now a somatic psychotherapist and mindful leadership consultant, I am unwilling to stand by quietly and do nothing while the world falls apart in front of my daughter's eyes. I have taken the grief and outrage from my experience of emotional abuse in a toxic co-parenting relationship, as well as an awareness of the moral outrage and burnout crisis facing educators, and I have transformed it into the wellness-based pathway laid out here.

The practices offered come from secular, research-backed programs, such as Somatic Psychotherapy and Family Systems modalities, Mindfulness-Based Cognitive Therapy (MBCT), Mindfulness-Based Stress Reduction (MBSR), Trauma-Sensitive Mindfulness, and Nonviolent Communication (NVC), and are informed by conversations and sessions with hundreds of parents, teachers, school leaders, domestic violence survivors, and my own trauma-healing journey.

If you are a people-pleaser in this isolating post-pandemic world, you are probably exhausted, lonely, overwhelmed, scared of what the future holds, and feeling like you can't do anything that really makes a difference. In your personal and professional relationships, you may be on the receiving end of anger, bitterness, resentment, hurt, and hatred, because no one is coping well, and we're all taking it out on each other. You might be taking the blame for problems that are way beyond the scope of any one person to address or taking on the responsibility for healing generations of trauma all on your own.

The challenges ahead of us are real and they are enormous. But we don't have to heal all of our ancestral wounds in one lifetime, and allowing ourselves to become buried by grief and overwhelm isn't going to help either. There is no one size fits all solution or quick fix, so right now I'd like to invite you to simply pause for a moment and breathe.

Take a full breath, all the way in and all the way out. Acknowledge the weight you are carrying, and that the pain and suffering you are personally experiencing is very real and deserves care and attention. Place a hand on your heart. Feel the rising and falling of your chest. Whisper to yourself, "I'm here. I'll take care of you."

If you are reading these words right now, **you are the ones we have been waiting for.** You care enough to have an influence on the people around you, and with this care channeled in the right direction, you *can* transform your relationship to yourself and to your community. You can have an impact in the larger system by prioritizing wellbeing for yourself, and by setting the intention to shift out of fear and reactivity using proven and practical skills to regulate your nervous system and be the port in the storm. You can commit to slowing down enough to pay attention to what is unfolding right now, and to speaking up for our rights to individual and collective healing. You can do these things because you are worth it. Our children are worth it. Humanity is worth it.

Together, we must embrace our relational wounding. We must be willing to see that we cannot create safety with fear-based thinking. Connection and caring are at the heart of how we heal, and if those in positions of influence can identify with this from a place of our own personal healing, perhaps we can together move one step closer to placing wellbeing and mental fitness at the center of our societal values, educational policies, and cultural identity.

We are living in some of the most trying times in the history of humanity, and the future of the planet itself depends upon how we re-imagine our relationships to ourselves and each other and embrace the changes we must make together. We must educate ourselves and the next generation in these practical skills for slowing down and learning to pay attention, so that we can all collaboratively engage in decisive action with calm, focused awareness.

Our children, more than previous generations, will need embodied leaders with fierce boundaries who can model resilience and mental fitness, skills for coping with immense difficulty, and with the capacity to lead with love, even amid great suffering. And just like anything that really matters, we must start this reckoning within ourselves.

Guidelines for Safety in Trauma Healing Work

The following guidelines will help you start to safely assert your boundaries right away, and they'll be fleshed out in more detail as we deepen into this work. Give them a try, even if doing so is new, uncomfortable, or feels risky, and see what changes as you lean into these practices a little more each day.

1. Stay in choice. Take care of yourself and take agency, whenever you notice that you are feeling compromised, frustrated, or trapped. Practice acting in the interest of your own wellbeing and speaking up for yourself even when it goes against the established social norms. For example, if you notice that your body is cramping and tense while you are sitting in a meeting, give yourself permission to change position, stretch, or stand while continuing to participate. If you're in conflict or under pressure to act quickly, give yourself a moment to take a sip of water and a full in and out breath before speaking or responding.

2. Be the conductor of your attention and reclaim your mental real estate. Practice bringing your attention to the present moment through mindfulness and sensory awareness. Train your nervous system to pause before jumping into fight/flight/freeze or reactivity. Build neural pathways during periods of stability that strengthen your mental fitness and increase your capacity to respond from a resourced home base of non-judgment and present-moment experience.

3. Focus on what's already working. Keep a gratitude journal, list simple pleasures, name the basic needs that are already being met, practice appreciation and loving kindness every day. This practice counteracts our instinctual negativity bias, and this is the antidote for catastrophic thinking, stress, and anxiety. With regular practice of bringing awareness to small moments of pleasure, it's possible to retrain your brain to focus more easily on what is right and what is already working, rather than what is wrong.

4. Keep your body and emotions moving. Moving helps us discharge stored traumatic energy, keeps pathways open for physical expression of big emotions, *and* releases dopamine and serotonin (the "happiness chemicals" in our brains). Externalize your feelings by expressing them outside of your body through nature play, exercise, dance, yoga, art, journaling, and music.

5. Be a strict gatekeeper of what you are taking in. Bring awareness to all the things you are taking in, including media, food and beverages, intoxicants, literature, the judgment of others, negative self-talk, air pollutants, and visual stimuli. Make an intentional commitment to allow only those substances, sources of information, and opinions that support nourishing your wellbeing to take up space in your mind. Avoid anything that adds more stress into your system or creates a negative feedback loop. Plan ahead of time and set boundaries as an investment in your future self. For example, when you are at the grocery store, avoid buying processed foods, and purchase ingredients for healthy salads and smoothies instead.

6. Don't engage in the drama unless you are fully in the driver's seat of what you are saying. Quick, fiery reactions often lead to regrets and can never truly be taken back. Only respond to toxic communications if you feel resourced, and if what you are offering comes from a place of careful discernment and your words are helpful and kind. Also, check in with your tendency to be an enabler. Chronic over-helping can prevent a codependent person from learning that they have the strength to help themselves and can actually keep them trapped.

You Are Not Alone

One thing I want to offer you right away, as you dive into this material, is gratitude. Thank you for caring enough about yourself and your relationships to bring attention to the repair that is needed. You are in the right place. Healing begins when you slow down and welcome yourself as you already are, without judgment, right here in the present moment. *At the core of systemic trauma is a deeply fractured relationship with ourselves.* It is in doing the work of repairing this relationship that we can begin to heal this core wound – that of belonging in our own bodies.

Life can be complicated and overwhelming, especially if you've experienced, or are still enmeshed in relational trauma. If there is ongoing threat and reactivity in your life, you may feel like you have reached your breaking point or as if you are living in crisis mode. At times, it simply becomes too much for the heart to bear. Your body may feel broken, your spirit, frazzled, and your soul, tired. Your nervous system may be completely overwhelmed, and you might even be creating storms with your hyper-vigilance, constantly anticipating triggers and threats before they even happen, feeling like you are always tiptoeing around on eggshells and broken glass.

Throughout this book, we'll explore a number of ways to rewire your brain, manage reactivity, and cultivate a sense of belonging within your own experience. But for right now, my invitation to you is to start simple — right here in the present moment, allowing yourself to be good enough, just as you are. **You are not broken, and you do not need to be fixed**. You are worthy of your own attention. When you pick up this book or listen to the guided practices, allow it to be a refuge for you, and give yourself the gift of this time when you don't have to go anywhere else, or accomplish anything, and there is no need to be anything for anyone. Experiment with giving yourself permission to welcome yourself, without having to change anything, and practice bringing care and attention to the experience you are already having of being an imperfect human.

When difficulty arises with these practices, know that this is completely normal. Rather than trying to avoid difficulty, see if you can lean in a little bit, and allow what arises to be information. When we ask, *what is this trying to teach me,* we have an opportunity to shed some light on our deeply patterned ways of doing things that are no longer serving us. It is from the muck of this inquiry that the lotus blossoms. The seed of healing is already within us, as is our natural inclination towards individuation, and growth. It is our birthright to create our own story, and to come home to the essence of ourselves that is alive in the wellspring of our soul from the very moment we are conceived. All it needs is the light of awareness, willingness to do it differently than our ancestors, and to inquire — *how is this situation inviting me to learn and grow?*

One of the reasons that our relationships are so difficult and characterized by great pain and suffering is that our grief comes from a place of tremendous love. All of us are grieving on some level. So many of us have experienced deep wounds to our sense of safety and belonging, and the resulting shame that we often internalize leads us to hide our pain, exile our feelings, and suffer in silence. Relational trauma can be unbearably lonely. The reality of the world we live in is that we are pressured and conditioned to keep going even amid ongoing grief. And we are likely doing so caught in a habit loop and protective strategies that were imprinted on our DNA by many generations of traumatized ancestors.

It may feel overwhelming and hopeless, but there is good news. First, if you've gotten ahold of this book, you now have access to therapeutic tools for working with overwhelm that are truly quite simple in their application. Once you have them in your toolkit, these skills can be accessed even during parenting challenges, full-blown arguments, crisis, and loss, and they are teachable at all ages. Second, your brain can change and grow, and what you put your attention towards flourishes. You can strengthen your capacity to attend to what is arising in the present moment and retrain yourself to be calm, grounded, and able to respond skillfully in the very moment that the need arises. Third, if you can learn to accept the things you can't control and control the things you can, you can start to create healthy boundaries with small, proactive changes in your own life and take baby steps that will improve your mental health and overall wellbeing and ripple outwards and positively impact many people around you.

So, before we dive in, I want to reiterate that you aren't alone and it's not your fault. Just like everyone else, you are a human being doing the best you can with the tools you have available, and the strategies you are using right now to survive and protect yourself make sense given all you've been through. Healing is possible and within reach, and you deserve care and attention, even if you have made mistakes.

Notice what it is like to read and consider these words. Become aware of sensations in the body, noticing areas of constriction, softening, bracing, or tensing. Bring curiosity to these sensations, getting to know them with kindness and non-judgment, not trying to make them go away, but rather getting interested in them. You might even place a hand on your heart, or offer yourself some other gesture of care, welcoming what arises as best you can.

This feeling is a part of you. This feeling belongs.

Are you Ready to Get Fierce? How to Use this Book

Boundaries help us set limits, differentiate ourselves, and provide physical and emotional safety, but they are not rigid walls meant to isolate us and keep everything out. They are more like gates of discernment that can be opened and closed to allow us to stay in choice and to connect and interact with others safely and with agency. Being the gatekeeper of your boundaries is what allows you the space to reclaim and restore yourself even in the wake of complex and systemic trauma. *You* hold the keys, and *you* get to be in charge of what comes in and what goes out. *You* get to make the rules and assert yourself, even when the whole world is trying to break through your defenses.

My hope is that the chapters that follow will help you find the courage to pick up that gate key and turn inwards, towards your heart and mind, and embrace the difficulties you face in your own way. Being firmly in the driver's seat of your experience can help you build capacity to make caring and compassionate choices, prioritize your wellbeing, and communicate your boundaries skillfully.

Part 1 includes attentional training exercises and resourcing activities that serve as a foundation for calming your nervous system and cultivating your inner awareness. You'll start by developing some skills for stabilizing attention and bringing a spirit of kind inquiry into your relationship to yourself. Becoming the master of your own mind and recognizing the signals from your body will serve as a home base for diving into the deeper waters of recognizing your habitual patterns and the places in your life where you may need to reconsider and reassert your boundaries.

Part 2 moves into the landscape of the heart and our habitual patterns and offers tools for acknowledging grief and the impact of relational trauma and for cultivating emotional literacy and responsivity. The practices offered here support caring for yourself amid difficulty, navigating conflicts with self-compassion, identifying and working with the imprint of attachment wounds, and flipping the script on self-critical and destructive thinking. This section also includes field-tested practices for interrupting trauma cycles and somatic exercises for externalizing grief, expressing anger, and releasing undischarged traumatic energy. We'll conclude with specific techniques and reflections to help you embody this recommitment to yourself so that you can continue to set and reset fierce and effective boundaries with clarity and compassion.

Somatic exercises and mindfulness practices are provided for each chapter, accompanied by journal and reflection prompts. As an investment in your future self, I recommend you purchase a notebook or journal where you can record your thoughts as you read and do the exercises. You'll be invited to come home to your body again and again, to learn from your own experience, and to rinse and repeat as many times as you need to so that these skills and new ways of relating to yourself can become integrated into your daily life.

The downloadable audio practices that accompany the text are available at fierceboundaries.com, and range from 3 minutes in length to 30. This is a marathon, not a sprint, so plan to space out this work in a way that is manageable for you, as lasting change does not happen overnight, and there are no quick fixes for systemic trauma.

You will get out of this work what you put into it, and you'll experience maximum benefit if you can carve out some time for daily practice. Our modern lives are characterized by time- and financial-scarcity, and a deeply engrained narrative that achievement, wealth, and status take precedence over wellbeing. Carving out time for your mental health is a radical act, one that has the power to change the world. You have to make time for your wellness, or you'll be forced to make time for your illness. This must be done in real time, rather than as a spectator, and takes effort and action. Just as you cannot learn how to play basketball by reading about it or watching a film, you cannot learn how to set healthy boundaries without cultivating inner awareness and responsivity first.

Trust me. It is not selfish, and it is not neglecting others to set boundaries so that you can pause and reset your nervous system a few times each day. You can even schedule this time on your calendar, and build it into your day as a non-negotiable, just as if it is a required meeting with an important colleague. Even if you can only pause for a moment, give yourself the gift of full your attention during this time. If you choose to practice while you are at work, or while you are tending to kids at home (which I highly recommend), you may wish to hang a "do not disturb" sign on your door or to let others know that you are occupied and not to be disrupted. Or better yet, invite your co-workers, partner, and kids to join you!

While the pathway to healing is not necessarily linear, the exercises in this book have been organized in an intentional sequence designed to support a safe healing journey. I highly recommend reading the chapters in the order in which they are presented and taking some time to digest and practice between chapters. Of course, you are welcome to skip ahead if that is your preference. However, please understand the importance of becoming firmly grounded in the present moment before investigating difficult experience. There is an overwhelming tendency amongst trauma survivors to over-attend to traumatic stimuli and become enmeshed in their traumatic memories. This is not useful if we are to truly integrate our experience and heal our relationship to ourselves.

In being willing to embrace your whole being, you are already creating a container and protecting your right to healing. *Healing is integration over time*, not a straight line from "broken" to "fixed." Healing doesn't mean getting things back to the way they were before you were hurt, rather it means reconditioning yourself so that you can be responsive from moment to moment and meet whatever arises with compassion and without abandoning your heart. With care and intention, it is possible to make space for traumatic or painful experiences within your narrative in such a way that your moments of grief and pain can serve as steppingstones from one time in your life to another, but no longer cause dysregulation or distress in your day-to-day life.

So now, I welcome you to embrace a new way of being with yourself, and to shift how you relate to being alive. Thank you for taking this opportunity to create new habits that invite pausing, slowing down, allowing, and meeting what is arising with presence and compassion. Thank you for your willingness to speak up for your right to peace, happiness, rest, safety, and whole-systems wellbeing. This is the kind of wisdom, leadership, and care that is so desperately needed. So, take all the time you need. You are worth it.

Part I:

Regulate. Resource.
Rest. Repeat.

Chapter 1: Come Home to Yourself

One of the biggest challenges in boundary setting is having the awareness to know *what* you need so that you can articulate it effectively. This can be especially difficult if you are a chronic people-pleaser, or if you are accustomed to numbing and dissociating and tuning out as a way of coping with difficulty, the way so many of us are. As a society, we have been systematically trained away from knowing what we need, much less asking for what we need, because we have lost our ability to connect with our felt experience and our inner knowing. We are encouraged instead to blast through our moments on the way to bigger and better moments, and along the way we miss important signals from our body that could help us take better care of our hearts and minds.

Have you ever noticed the prickle on the back of your neck when something isn't right, or you are in danger? How about a churning in your stomach when you've made a mistake, or you are uncomfortable in an interaction? Or maybe you've noticed a sinking feeling in your chest when there is loss or disappointment, or a flushing of heat in your cheeks and a clenching of your fists when you are angry? The body knows what we need faster than we can formulate a rational thought and articulate a request. But we are conditioned to ignore these symptoms of imbalance and dis-ease, or even to treat them with medication and to look for solutions to our discomfort outside of ourselves.

We live in a fast-paced corporatized world that capitalizes from keeping us on the hamster wheel — multi-tasking, over-working, and prioritizing achievement, image, and material wealth over our physical and emotional wellbeing. It makes sense that we are chronically exhausted and experiencing growing levels of depression, anxiety, and interpersonal violence. Additionally, with the prevalence of our social media and smartphones, we have become addicted to shifting our attention quickly from one image to the next, to zoning out while we scroll mindlessly, and to escaping our reality by bingeing, numbing, and endlessly consuming. Big business and big pharma want us to disregard our body's knowing because when we fail to pay attention to our depletion and our outrage, then we stay hooked and spend more money. We buy products, medications, and subscriptions to mask our gaping wounds of feeling like strangers in our own skin.

The body holds so much wisdom that we often ignore when we are living in our heads. Chronic pain and tension in the body are often indicators of a systemic imbalance and are the physiological expression of psychological distress. For example, back pain may be indicative of carrying a heavy emotional burden or a tension headache may be the result of financial stress or pressure to perform. Gut trouble or digestion issues may be the physical signal that what we are taking in relationally is filling us with toxicity. When we are willing to slow down and pay attention to the information that is available from the body, then we can start to explore what we truly need. Once we know what we need, it becomes much easier to set a boundary and to make a clear and effective request to get our needs met.

The foundation of this work will be the practices of *somatic awareness* and *mindfulness*, which when brought together can be effective interventions for regulating and repairing a traumatized nervous system.

Somatic - *Soma* means "body" in Greek, so *somatic* means "of the body." *Somatic awareness* practices simply refer to those that access the wisdom of the body and the inherent intelligence of our nervous system, *rather* than focusing on cognitive knowing or thoughts.

Mindfulness - Paying attention to what is happening in the present moment, with kindness and curiosity. Mindfulness practices include mental fitness and attentional training as well as an attitude of allowing ourselves to *be just as we are* right now, without judgment. Mindfulness is simple and available to anyone, anytime, and can be a very effective practice for making permanent habit changes, reducing anxiety, and improving overall wellbeing.

Mindfulness *is not* always easy or a quick fix for any problem. It does *not* necessarily mean stopping your thoughts or finding "inner peace" and it is *not* inherently religious or for everyone, as it may be contraindicated if you are experiencing acute traumatic arousal, recent grief, active substance use, and some mental disorders.

You don't have to go anywhere or do anything special to cultivate somatic awareness or to experience the benefit of mindfulness. You don't need a special bell or cushion or to go on a long retreat, or even to sit for long periods of time in silent meditation. All you need to have access to is your own body and the willingness to pay attention to it in a nonjudgmental and caring way. This is an invitation to embrace a quality of *being* and belonging, rather than *doing* or having to accomplish a fixed outcome. These exercises and skills can be incorporated into everyday life, called upon in moments of stress reactivity, conflict, or major life decisions, and can be accessed to help you reset and regroup when you get knocked off-balance.

Healing through somatic awareness and mindfulness requires us to believe in the body-mind connection and to *slow down* enough to notice what is happening in our felt experience. For many people this first step is often the most difficult and the most necessary.

Letting *Go* vs. Letting *Be*

In toxic workplaces, where people are under tremendous pressure and are often so anxious that intrusive thoughts keep them from sleeping at night, there are severe consequences for failing to comply, conform, and meet the often-unrealistic expectations of their employers. It can feel impossible to care for yourself while also keeping your job intact, and the worry thoughts and list of tasks can run on an endless loop unless you have honed some skills for tuning them out. Many of us believe that if we were to take time to rest in the middle of our workday, or schedule an extended vacation or mental health day, we would likely be looked down upon, laughed at, and otherwise judged. "Down time" is laziness and doing "nothing" is slacking off. And we're indoctrinated to think that taking time for self-care means that our responsibilities will be neglected, the workload will pile up, that we will be perceived as selfish or entitled, and depending upon who notices, we may even be fired.

To slow down the spiral of anxiety and stressful thoughts, we are casually told to simply **"let it go,"** but we are never effectively taught *how* to do this. Besides, the threat to our belonging and livelihood is often very real. In fact, when anxiety escalates into worrying about what other people think, and you believe that you need to hide your exhaustion, ignore your grief, suppress your anger, and pull yourself together, guess what happens? You fall apart. When someone tells you to "calm down," the volcano erupts. When someone asks, "what's wrong?" the dam bursts. Then, there's a much bigger mess to clean up.

Anxiety is often rooted in deep fear of our unworthiness and is a clear message from our system that something needs to change, or we won't survive. It is a wound to our safety and belonging, and when we don't tend to this wound or pour salt in it with the fear that someone might see us falling apart, it only exacerbates our feeling of panic. When that thought train is barreling down the track at full speed, our eyes are darting around and our heart is racing, it seems impossible to stop it. We are certain, and our nervous system believes, that we are headed off the cliff of certain doom.

The socially accepted remedy for widespread anxiety and panic is to medicate and numb ourselves into rest. We are encouraged to turn off the never-ending worthiness and threat alarm by drinking alcohol at the end of the day or to tune out by watching television or scrolling social media. The only way many of us know how to disentangle ourselves from the parts of our lives that we resent and fear, and that haunt us in the waking hours after midnight, is to go away from ourselves, to distance ourselves from our own experience, and to drown our authenticity with things that make us forget who we are.

But what if instead of leaving ourselves and tuning out, we practiced tuning *in*. What if instead of trying to forget, we learned how to *remember* ourselves and come home to our bodies after a long day. What if instead of trying to "let go," we practiced letting ourselves *be,* just as we already are, tired, messy, angry, scared, lonely, hungry humans.

I'd like to invite you to consider a new definition for the word "remember" — the opposite of "dismember," meaning to remove parts of the body. What if when we remember ourselves, we put our bodies back together and take up residency in them? What if remembering ourselves meant sensing into the felt experience of our arms, legs, hands, feet, pelvis, chest, and face? By tending to sensations in the body, just as they are, and cultivating this capacity for physical literacy, we can offer ourselves an alternative to thinking our feelings and create a landscape where it is possible to investigate, allow, and *be with* our feelings with curiosity and care.

I invite you to try the following somatic experiment. You can also find a 3-minute audio recording of this exercise at fierceboundaries.com.

Exercise 1.1: Fist Experiment

Make a fist with one hand, imagining that the job of this fist is to stay closed. Notice what happens in your body as you do this.

Now, with the opposite hand, try to pry the fist open, remembering that the job of the fist is to stay closed. Notice what happens in the body now.

Then, take a breath and release the fist, taking a moment to shake out both hands, letting go of that experience.

Now, make a fist again, perhaps with the other hand this time. Once again, the job of this fist is to stay closed.

This time, instead of trying to pry the fist open, the opposite hand is going to come underneath the fist and cradle it. Notice what happens in

---

the body when you do this.

Finally, you might even imagine that the cradling hand is helping the fist stay closed. Notice what happens now.

Take a breath and release the fist, shaking out the hands, and letting go of that practice.

Reflection: What did you notice when you tried to pry the fist open? What did you notice when you cradled the fist? How might this practice support you in welcoming yourself?

The Power of Allowing

The previous somatic exercise[1] was first offered to me by David Treleaven, the author of the book, *Trauma Sensitive Mindfulness*. He adopted it from Staci Haines' teachings on trauma, somatics, and social justice (2019). Since then, it has become the backbone of my work with educators and survivors of relational trauma.

I do this experiment with almost everyone who comes to me for therapy and even with large groups of students, young and old. Every time I do it, I am struck by the impact of this simple somatic exercise. While you may have had a different experience than others, most participants report that it does not feel good to try to pry the fist and that they become aware of anxiety, frustration, and an increase in tension when they do so. In cradling the fist, on the other hand, many people report the softening of the fist and a wave of emotion. Often, when they share this reflection, there are some tears and a feeling of connection in the room as other participants nod and confirm that they noticed something similar.I do this experiment with almost everyone who comes to me for therapy and even with large groups of students, young and old. Every time I do it, I am struck by the impact of this simple somatic exercise. While you may have had a different experience than others, most participants report that it does not feel good to try to pry the fist and that they become aware of anxiety, frustration, and an increase in tension when they do so. In cradling the fist, on the other hand, many people report the softening of the fist and a wave of emotion. Often, when they share this reflection, there are some tears and a feeling of connection in the room as other participants nod and confirm that they noticed something similar.

This experiment offers us two essential questions at the heart of somatic awareness practices that we can ask ourselves amid difficulty: 1. *What is arising in my present moment experience? 2. How can I best care for myself, given what is arising?* Prying the fist open is the equivalent of exiling an emotion and trying to simply "let it go" or to ignore it. However, the emotion is real, holds information about what is needed, and has an important job to do to keep us safe. Every signal from the body is valid, and there is no part of us that is bad or deserves to be pried apart, isolated, or silenced. When we cradle the fist instead, and even help it to stay closed, this makes space for our emotions without pathologizing them. Multiple layers of healing can happen when we *allow* ourselves to have the experience we are having, honor our humanness, and welcome our wounded parts back from exile.

Here is a story from my teaching days about exiling and allowing: One day, I pulled into the school parking lot, and suddenly, I couldn't breathe. My chest seized and contracted, my hands started to tremble violently, and sweat poured down my back. It wasn't my first panic attack, but it was the worst one I'd had yet, and the timing was extremely inconvenient, because I was already late for work.

By the time I managed to regain enough composure to walk into the school building, it was already well into homeroom. The look slung at me by the covering teacher reiterated everything my inner critic was already shouting inside me, *I sucked. I couldn't do anything right. I was unprofessional and too much! Why did they ever hire a loser like me? I was not anywhere near good enough to deserve this swanky corner classroom with windows.*

Later, standing in front of the whiteboard during second period, trying in vain to quiet and gain the attention of 29 eighth graders, I felt my frustration build. Hot pressure pushed at my temples. Watching me sputter with anger, a few students giggled, and something flew across the room.

Then, like a volcanic explosion, the lava of my emotions boiled over. After a brief, non-sensical tirade, I collapsed wordlessly into my chair and buried my head in my arms, red-faced and crying. This was not the teacher I wanted to be. It took only a few seconds for my astonished students to fall dead silent. With my head down and my body heaving, I felt completely broken and incapable of doing the job that I loved so dearly. *I had let everyone down by falling apart. I had failed my students and myself.*

After a few moments, I looked up through my blur of tears, and saw the wide, concerned eyes of my students. The scene in front of me startled me to attention. I realized, suddenly, that I was contagious. My own emotional and mental state had created the chaotic climate in the classroom, and we were all experiencing the effects of my dysregulation and lack of self-care together. I had been working so hard to hide my inner turmoil, to suppress my pain, and to ignore my feelings to keep my job, and to be the good teacher they all deserved, that I had unknowingly cultivated an environment that was alienating, anxious, unstable, and volatile, just like my shattered nervous system.

"I'm sorry you guys," I said.

"What's wrong, Ms. Cindy?" a student asked, softly.

I took a deep breath, and then finally let the truth spill out. I told them about my failed marriage, my back pain, my fear of losing my job, how anxious and scared I was, how hard it was to be a single mother of a toddler, how I worried about my ex's mental health all the time, and how divorcing him felt like my best friend had died. I told them about my panic attacks in the morning, how I was always scrambling, and struggling to show up as their teacher. "I am so sorry I have let you all down."

I glanced around the room and saw multiple students whose eyes were red and filled with tears, and I passed out tissues.

One student, a boy named Garrett who was one of my biggest behavioral challenges, stood up and said, "We love you, Ms. Cindy. This is my favorite class, and you're the best teacher I've ever had." Then he walked towards the front of the classroom and wrapped his arms around me. Other students joined him, and I was smothered by a giggly, awkward group hug.

"Can we watch a movie now?" one student said, and everyone laughed. (They knew that this was no longer allowed in my class without prior parent approval as per a recent decree from administration).

"Let's play vocab bingo," I said, laughing and wiping the tears from my face. A collective cheer erupted from the group.

For the rest of the week, they showered me with praise and words of encouragement. Behavior and grades improved, and students even turned in their homework without being badgered about it. One by one, they also started to approach me during lunch and after class, and to share with me their struggles with eating disorders, sexual identity, addiction, stories about their parents who divorced or were about to, asking for advice about relationships in which they were being bullied, and seeking help with navigating violent home situations. When I came back from lunch, my desk was often covered in hand-written notes, gifts of candy, cute drawings, and anonymous reports of concern for students who needed support but wouldn't or couldn't ask for it.

By giving myself permission to have the difficult and messy experience I was already having, and to name my emotions and welcome them, a ripple of healing and connection had pulsed through our classroom community. Prior to my emotional breakdown, when I was still determined to hide my anxiety for the sake of professionalism and being a good teacher, I would have characterized my classroom environment as overwhelming, unmanageable, impossible to handle, and full of behavior problems and "at risk" students. After sharing my struggles, and because I finally gave myself permission to be authentic, the atmosphere shifted to one of care, connection, and growing together in a classroom community.

This is not to say that if you are having behavioral problems or disciplinary challenges that you should break down and have a panic attack in front of your kids or colleagues. In fact, my panic attack happened because I had not been honoring my needs, setting effective boundaries, or tending to myself and as a result I had reached a breaking point. I was carrying too much that didn't belong to me, refusing to say no for fear of being fired or rejected, and ignoring all the warning signs my body was giving me that something had to change.

As I reflected on the unraveling of my mental and emotional state over the following days, I realized that the more I suppressed and ignored my authentic human experience and exiled my emotions for the sake of others, the more my distress grew and festered inside me. Moving forward, I tried listening to the signals my nervous system was sending me a little bit more. I stopped pretending to be super-human and let myself just be the messy, disorganized, last-minute-lesson-planning, imperfect, human full of grief and stress that I was. Astonishingly, students were more engaged, performed better, and behaved differently, with a new sense of care and mutual respect at the heart of most of our interactions. Even Garrett was more cooperative and soon became one of my star students.

To help me manage my chaotic life a little better, I downloaded a mindfulness app on my phone with a handful of guided practices that were just a few minutes long, making a commitment to squeeze these in between classes so that I could get better at regulating myself. As soon as the bell rang at the end of class, I shuffled my students out and locked the door. I had a luxurious seven minutes, which was just enough time to listen to a 3-minute recording and for a trip to the bathroom.

For a few stolen moments at a time, I practiced focusing on my breath, or sounds, or an object, while students yanked on the door handle and peered through the window, saying "she's in there, I can see her… but the door's locked." They weren't used to me prioritizing myself over them.

Soon, I developed strategies to protect these precious minutes of tending to my own wellbeing. I made a sign for the door that said, "do not disturb," and acclimated the students to the new routine of waiting outside the classroom quietly until I opened the door and let them in.

Setting that boundary for myself, pausing to listen to these recordings, and the mini moments of stabilizing my attention with an anchor, instantly made a difference. With just three minutes of guidance and focused attention that supported me in slowing down, calming my nervous system, and bringing awareness into the sensations in my body, my attitude and mood shifted and everything about my classroom and emotional wellbeing changed. These resets gave me the opportunity to find a resting place and begin again, even if only for a few minutes.

I even started being able to apply these skills during class, and to pause and ground myself automatically, whenever I noticed anxiety returning. I was less reactive, less emotionally exhausted, more resourced, and one breath at a time, the students started to get their devoted teacher back. The combination of allowing myself to be less than perfect and fiercely protecting my three-minute pauses became the lifeboat that carried me through the rest of the school year.

Put Out the Welcome Mat

Welcoming yourself to belong within your own experience is powerful medicine. Basic mindfulness practice offers us the opportunity to do this in a very specific way, by bringing attention to rest on an anchor in the present moment and allowing ourselves to investigate what arises. In essence, it is a way of giving ourselves the gift of our own attention, and "putting out the welcome mat" for ourselves.

For the following exercise, we'll explore different anchors by shifting our attention with intention from one anchor to another. This is a seated practice suitable for beginners who have never done mindfulness meditation before, and one that you can use at any time of day to help you ground attention and cultivate body awareness and presence. For these next few minutes, there is no need to be anything for anyone, or to get anything done, just give yourself permission to be worthy of your own attention, and to let that be enough.

Abbreviated instructions are provided for this practice here and a 10-minute guided audio is available at fierceboundaries.com. While it is possible to do this practice while reading these instructions, listening to the recording will give you the chance to attend to yourself more fully.

Exercise 1.2: Introductory Mindfulness Practice

Adopt an upright **posture** and bring the feet flat down to the floor. Notice the sensations of gravity and pressure in the body. You can close the eyes if it feels comfortable, or you can just rest the eyes in a soft, downward gaze.

Bring attention to the **sensations of the breath**. Notice the movement of air into and out of the body and feel the rising and falling of the chest. You might notice the sensations of air entering the nostrils and hitting the back of the throat, or the expansion and contraction of your rib cage. Wherever you most notice the breath, rest attention here.

If attention is pulled into thoughts, planning, or activity in your environment, know that this is completely normal. Notice this movement of mind, and without judgment, guide attention back to the sensations of the breath. The objective of this practice is not to stop thoughts, but to strengthen attentional control by bringing attention back to the intended area of focus.

Now, release attention from the sensations of breath, and shift up to the ears, **attending to sounds**. Notice sounds that are close and farther away, inside the room and outside the room, letting sounds come and go. Again, if attention shifts, gently guide it back to receiving sound.

Now, shift your attention towards **sensations in the body**. You might notice areas of tension, bracing, or holding, or you might notice sensations of pressure. There is no need to change the body or create any special feelings or sensations, this is simply a time to be with the body you already have.

When you are ready, bring the attention back to the breath, taking a full inhale and exhale as you release this practice. Invite some gentle movement into the body, and blink open the eyes if they've been closed, bringing this moment-to-moment welcoming of your own experience into the next moments of your day.

Reflection: What did you notice during that practice? You might have experienced sensations, thoughts, feelings, sounds, or attention being pulled in many directions. What is it like to pay attention to your present-moment experience in this way?

Chapter 2: Know Your Nervous System

O ur brains evolved to survive in a very different world than the one we live in today. It has been thousands of years since we left our humble caveman roots and leapt on the fast train of achievement, status, and wealth. When we started to organize in sedentary communities and develop power structures that separated us into classes, we planted the seeds for modern capitalism and for our quest to have and be more. We now experience a never-ending race to the top, widespread societal illness, environmental imbalance, and increasing time indoors and separated from the natural world that was once our home.

However, our wiring is still the same as it was when we lived in small traveling bands. The autonomic nervous system (ANS) is made up of two branches originally designed to navigate the hostile conditions of the savannah:

Sympathetic: The sympathetic nervous system governs our survival responses. When the sympathetic branch is activated, the body mobilizes for attack (fight) or escape (flight). If neither of these tactics are successful, we become immobilized (freeze) as if to play dead or avoid detection.

Parasympathetic. The parasympathetic nervous system governs our "rest and digest" and "feed and breed" responses. When we are in a state of parasympathetic activation, our heartrate is steady and rhythmic, our digestion is regulated, and we feel a sense of safety and rest.

Perhaps you have noticed that when you are feeling anxious, stressed, or fearful that your vision narrows, your stomach grinds to a standstill, and it can be hard to think clearly? This is because when you are in survival mode or experiencing a threat, your sympathetic nervous system is activated, and stress hormones are dumped into your bloodstream.

Now, imagine that you are an early human, walking across the savannah, and you get a prickle of fear at the back of your neck, and the sense that there is a predator stalking you. Your senses go on high alert as you scan for threat. You may notice the twitch of a blade of grass, or a small, subtle movement out of the corner of your eye. Your muscles tense, and instantly your body's survival response kicks into high gear. Your **amygdala** (a part of the brain that detects threat) sends a signal to the hypothalamus, which releases adrenaline and cortisol into your blood stream.

During this period of activation, the functions that are not needed for survival go off-line, including digestion and the **pre-frontal cortex** (PFC), which is responsible for choice, decision-making, impulse inhibition, and cognitive control. When the PFC shuts down, this energy is redirected towards mobilizing our defenses. Our hearing becomes more acute, our heart rate speeds up, and the blood flow to our limbs increases as we prepare to fight or flee.

So, if critical parts of our brain go off-line when we perceive a threat, it is no wonder that we can have trouble making good decisions when we feel angry, scared, or stressed. This also explains why when we are overwhelmed or under pressure, we are more prone to accidents, injury, and making mistakes. This was a very useful adaptation when we lived on the savannah. But now, we live in a world full of constant threat, hyper-productivity, and normalized anxiety, and many of us are walking around in a state of chronic sympathetic arousal.

It is important to also remember that in our earliest days of reacting to the occasional threat of tigers, or activating our physical energy to hunt large mammals, we had long periods in between threats of rest and digest mode. Parasympathetic arousal is the state in which our bodies are designed to reside. Our parasympathetic nervous system is meant to be our baseline — a state of regulation and rhythm that is optimal for restoring the body's resources, replenishing our reserves, and allowing us to relax into the safety and connection that is available within our relationships and family life.

We can activate the parasympathetic nervous system by orienting with our senses, taking deep and slow breaths, through rhythmic movement, physical touch, laughter, meditation, yoga, music, walks in nature, and engaging in pleasurable activities. Though modern humans do not often experience being chased by a tiger, our world is filled with threats that keep us from enjoying parasympathetic restoration. Additionally, when we experience a trauma or ongoing threat to ourselves or others, our sympathetic nervous systems may become reactive or stuck on "on." This can be experienced as anxiety, insomnia, chronic pain, hyper vigilance, high blood pressure, an exaggerated startle response, constant worry or rumination, compulsive aggression, attention deficit disorders, and other mental and physical health conditions that are the body's response to chronic tension and fear. This is happening on a widespread level in our schools, workplaces, institutions, and families, and as a society we are collectively experiencing higher levels of sympathetic nervous system arousal than our bodies are designed to handle.

Worse, many of the behaviors that keep us in a state of sympathetic arousal are celebrated within our culture and have become habitual and maladaptive, in such a way that they add even more stress into our lives as we seesaw between extremes, creating a negative feedback loop that keeps us on the roller coaster of unhealthy coping and catastrophizing.

Negativity Bias

The habit of worrying and over-focusing our attention on problems, threats, and future disasters makes sense considering the conditions within which our brains evolved. Our attention is naturally pulled towards what is potentially dangerous in our environment so that we can keep ourselves alive. *Perceived threat* activates the sympathetic nervous system in the same way an actual threat does, *and* threats to our sense of belonging are registered as just as hazardous to our survival as a predator crouched behind a bush ready to pounce. We are primed to notice the slight twitch of a blade of grass and the smallest hint of negative intonation in our partner's voice the same way.

The thing is, these are *perceived* threats based in our natural **negativity bias**, but often our life and belonging are not in immediate danger in the present moment.

Understanding Negativity Bias

Negativity Bias: Based in our early evolution, this is the tendency to attend to, learn from, and use negative information more than positive information. Negative experiences elicit a strong and rapid response, that was originally designed to detect threat and help us survive in a life-or-death environment.

> **Try this:** Bring to mind a recent situation when you felt good, happy, peaceful, loving, relaxed, or at ease. Notice the sensations that arise in your body. Can you name them? What do you feel physically as you explore your body for any signature of these pleasant emotions?
>
> Now, bring to mind a recent situation when you felt angry, upset, frightened, or disturbed. Again, notice the sensations that arise in your body. Can you name them? What do you feel physically as you explore your body for any signature of these unpleasant emotions?

It's likely that with the unpleasant experience in mind, there are some pretty strong sensations that come into awareness, such as clenching, bracing, tensing, churning, heat, or discomfort. Chances are that this negative information in your system is more noticeable than the pleasant experience was.

The reason unpleasant experiences are more noticeable is your inherent negativity bias, the body's way of letting you know something is wrong and needs immediate attention.

When we perceive that we are in danger, whether physically or relationally, we are designed to notice. Even though we may feel the symptoms of acute fear, panic, and reactivity, many of our modern threats aren't really endangering us at all right now in the present moment. The person we may be worried about letting down or offending isn't even in the room with us, or the bill we are concerned about paying isn't due for another few weeks. That thing that so-and-so said the other day that hurt our feelings is still spinning around in our minds, but that person isn't anywhere in sight. But it has our attention, and we stress and feel anxious anyway, sending our sympathetic nervous system into action over and over again.

Even if we do miss a payment or make a mistake, the world won't actually end, and we won't actually be eaten. It can be hard to remember this living in a traumatized world, governed by hypervigilance and perpetual fearmongering. As a culture, we exist in a state of collective and chronic fight/flight, and our bodies have become habituated to reacting to triggers as if there is predator around every bend in the road. Couple this with the uncertainty and unpredictability of the climate, prolific gun violence, discrimination, and the political world we live in, and you have a recipe for nervous system implosion at every turn. This chronicity of extreme stress has created widespread individual, societal, and systemic illness that feeds back on itself to over-tax our nervous systems and create conflict and reactivity in our relationships. Additionally, as if this level of chronic stress wasn't enough, fear-based thinking has become normalized in workplace and educational settings and safety, joy, connection, and positivity have been relegated to our free-time.

Furthermore, we can't set clear and consistent boundaries that keep us safe and grounded or connect from our hearts if we are perpetually looking over our shoulders for the next threat to our relational safety. For this reason, many of us tend to minimize our pleasant experiences, not just out of habit, but also for fear of overwhelming someone who is suffering.

In my own disastrous marriage, my ex-husband's depression cast a black cloud over everything. I got used to hiding my joy because when I expressed feeling good it only reminded him of how bad he felt in comparison. It didn't take long before I forgot how to be playful, to let loose, and to feel free to smile and laugh at the little things. I lost my light-heartedness because I felt badly about feeling good. I see this "survivor's guilt" all the time in my clients and in educators. We are afraid to express our happiness because it might compromise our belonging in relationships that are already unsafe to begin with. Since negativity bias is so deeply engrained in how the mind works, it's easy to become habituated to brushing over moments of pleasure, dismissing them, or even abandoning joy entirely for the sake of taking care of others who may be having a less pleasant experience trudging through their own lives.

We may even find that our moments of happiness are tainted by a sense of "foreboding joy," the feeling that the joy we are experiencing is too good to be true, and that if we are feeling good now, there must be some disaster or karmic retribution on the horizon. This is also a product of our cultural conditioning and reflects a widespread belief that we do not deserve to be happy while others are suffering, and that pleasure is sinful or selfish. This is especially common in codependent relationships and when we are trauma-bonded or intimately tied to someone with depression, narcissistic behaviors, mental or physical illness, or chronic pain.

Hack Your Body's Fear Response

The good news is that when we understand these basic mechanics of negativity bias and how the nervous system works, we can engage the brain in simple and counterintuitive practices that switch us out of habitual negative or fear-based thinking. One of the ways we can counteract chronic sympathetic arousal is to **spend intentional time activating the parasympathetic nervous system on purpose**, by attending to what's real and right in front of us, rather than focusing on our fears. With regular practice, we can even re-train our attention to return to a baseline of resting in what is good, safe, and nourishing. The more mental fitness we have in this area, the more resilient we are when faced with challenges.

Our sensory awareness and basic human functions are a very effective place to cultivate this kind of awareness of what is already working for us. Even in the face of uncertainty, there are parts of our experience we can always trust, such as our breath, gravity, and the fact that we have a body that is always moving towards healing and keeping us alive. A brief arrival in the present moment and momentarily shifting attention out of worrying about the future or ruminating about the past can down-regulate our amygdala and bring our pre-frontal cortex back online.

The most basic of these practices is to take a full and complete breath, feeling the air fill the lungs, expanding the diaphragm, and noticing the movement of air in the body. Think of it this way: If we were being chased by a real tiger, there would not be time to stop and take a full deep breath with awareness. So therefore, when we do slow down and bring our attention to our senses, we can essentially "hack" our stress-reactivity system and send our brain an instant message that there is no real and present danger.

In receiving this signal, the amygdala down-regulates and stops releasing stress hormones into the system, very quickly bringing our PFC back into operation and giving us the capacity to choose a response with all our faculties on-line.

Try the following exercise, using the acronym S.T.O.P., the next time that you notice yourself feeling stressed or reactive.

Exercise 2.1: S.T.O.P.

S. Stop what you are doing, notice that the moment is stressful.

T. Take a full breath, all the way in and out. Pay attention to the sensations of the breath.

O. Observe what is present, right now. Notice your inner and outer environment. Engage the senses and become aware of sensations in the body.

P. Proceed. Choose a response and continue with awareness.

A printable S.T.O.P. poster and a 3-minute "Press Pause" practice are also available at fierceboundaries.com

While it can take as much as 15 minutes for the parasympathetic nervous system to fully engage, the more we practice this skill, the more accessible it becomes, and the more we increase our resilience. We can increase our mental fitness and our capacity to stabilize attention in the midst of stress by regularly orienting to the present moment and focusing on any internal or external object of attention, such as the breath, movement in the body, the sound of a bell, a stone held in the hand, or even a tree or cloud outside of our window. Studies on long-term meditators and habit change show that we *can* change the chemistry of our brain, grow new neural pathways, decrease our startle response, and greatly improve our wellbeing with this kind of attentional training.

Neuroplasticity is the capacity of the brain to change and adapt due to experience and in response to new ways of directing our attention. These pathways are easiest to build when we are young, but we can build new neural pathways at any age, though it may take more time and energy as we get older.

I like to think of building neural pathways like making a new path in a dense, uncharted jungle. The first time we travel it, we must hack away a lot of branches and vines with our machete, and we may only make it a short distance before we get tired or frightened off by a poisonous snake. But if we are willing to return the next day and continue pruning, keeping a watchful eye out for danger, we might make a little more progress. Eventually, with repeated and regular efforts, we get to know where the snakes like to hide and can avoid them, and we will have a wide-open and clear path through this jungle that requires only occasional tending.

However, if we fail to travel this new pathway regularly, or give up before we have cleared the way to our intended destination, the vines and branches will quickly overgrow, the snakes will roam where they please, and there will no longer be a pathway at all causing us to have to start all over again. The phrase "use it, or lose it," aptly demonstrates this phenomenon. The synapses in our brain, which connect our intentions to our processes, are always being pruned if they aren't needed. The capabilities we are not using quickly recede, as anyone who has tried to learn a foreign language or studied calculus in college, but never used it, can tell you. Repetition and practice are the keys to learning. When you consistently direct your attention with intention and assert boundaries around where you choose to place your focus, you can reclaim pieces of yourself that you didn't even know were hijacked.

Try the following brief exercise:

Exercise 2.2: Ten Breaths

Pause, and see if you can focus your attention on your breath for the length of ten full inhales and exhales. Breathe in and out, without trying to control the breath or breathe in any special way.

Can you feel the sensations of air moving in through your nostrils? Or perhaps you notice the rising and falling of your chest, or the movement of your ribcage? How do you know you are breathing?

If your attention is pulled into thoughts or planning, don't worry! This is completely normal. When you notice this movement of mind, simply acknowledge that attention has shifted, and then gently guide it back to the sensations of breathing. Just this act of noticing is a moment of mindful awareness.

Reflection: How many times did your attention wander away from the breath? How many times did you bring it back?

Reclaim Your Attention

Don't feel badly about yourself if your mind wandered during that exercise. Minds wander! Their job is to think of things to think about and then to think some more. It's completely normal to experience the movement of mind, especially the first few times you attempt to rest your attention with an anchor such as the breath. Ten breaths is a lot, and it's a good number to use for your mental fitness training. Within the space created by ten full breaths, a lot of things can change. If ten feels like too many, or you're being hard on yourself for not being able to stay focused, simply start with attending to one full breath. See if you can hold attention with the sensations of breathing from the very beginning of an inhale all the way through the completion of the exhale. Slowly, one breath, three breaths, ten breaths at a time, you can build capacity to sustain your attention in the present moment for longer periods of time.

Reclaiming our attention and becoming the masters of our minds is a radical act of defiance against a corporatized system that profits from hijacking us and encouraging us to stay on the hamster wheel of overconsumption. When we are willing to set fierce boundaries around what we attend to and protect our mental real estate, we make a big leap in taking back our individual and collective power. By refusing to be numb, blind, and silent about the ways we are being hijacked and the harm that is being perpetuated on us, we can step firmly into the driver's seat of our own experience and begin the critical work of disentangling ourselves from the weight of systemic oppression, simply by training ourselves to pay attention.

When we have intrusive thoughts that keep us from thriving, or when our attention is hooked into ruminating about what happened in the past or worrying about what might happen in the future, we are robbed of our right to be present with what is unfolding right now. Not only do these intrusive thoughts keep us from experiencing life as it is unfolding, but they can contribute to reactivity and habitual patterns of bracing and tensing that lead to chronic pain, substance abuse, and relational conflict. When we are on autopilot, we can be so easily steered away from our authentic selves, and we forget who we are, get caught up in the turmoil, and lose sight of what truly matters.

Energy follows thought, and wherever we regularly place our attention, we will have well-traveled neural pathways and impulsively and automatically be pulled into behaviors and reactions that happen without awareness. You probably didn't mean to spend four hours watching TikTok videos, or to eat that entire package of cookies without realizing it, or to spend money you don't have on skin care products that promise to make you look younger and just end up cluttering your bathroom shelves.

Attention sells, and our worthiness is a commodity that has been usurped by the pharmaceutical industry and the modern media. We are battered from every angle with messages that we need to medicate and improve ourselves and be better looking or more fit, and to buy more products so we can attract love, look more beautiful, and feel better.

But, when we start this work within ourselves and take back our right to place our attention where it supports our wellbeing, we can then model these healthier coping strategies and be the change we wish to see in the world. What the world needs right now, more than wrinkle-free skin, is an army of mentally fit peaceful warriors, who are paying enough attention to act skillfully and respond effectively when their moment arises.

Chapter 3: Mastering Mental Fitness

Every time we direct our focus to an anchor in the present moment, notice that it has shifted away, and then bring it back, this is like lifting weights for the mind. We can strengthen our "attention muscle" by spending time training attention. Each act of noticing the movement of mind and bringing it back is like doing another "rep." This practice gives us an opportunity to become aware of where our attention is hooked, and then to place it where we want it. Over time, we can train ourselves in "mental fitness." This is critical in setting boundaries because it gives us the strength to unhook from our habitual patterns and the space to make an informed and calm choice about what is needed.

"Single tasking" is a mental fitness practice that involves doing just one thing with full awareness. It is the opposite of multitasking. Single tasking allows us to deepen our focus and to cultivate the ability to shift attention with intention from one part of our experience to another. We'll practice this skill by focusing on a *sensory anchor* in the present moment: bringing our attention toward sounds, the breath, seeing, and physical sensations, such as noticing gravity in the body or the movement of the breath. The senses are a great place to start because they are always with us, and they are also inherently happening in the present moment, without us having to do anything or accomplish anything special to access them.

As we progress, we'll shift our attention from one anchor to another, building our mental fitness and our capacity to be the conductor of our attention. Over time, regularly focusing your attention with the five senses can also increase your capacity for prolonged concentration, steadiness in the face of difficultly, and give you access to a deep source of body wisdom that you can call upon to guide you through the most challenging of times.

Single tasking allowed me to stabilize my attention, step out of automatic thought patterns, and come home to myself during some of the most challenging times of my life. I share these guided practices with you here because they were available and practical for me in a real-world context when I most needed regulation and didn't have time for extended periods of meditation. They are available anywhere, anytime, to anyone who has a body. My hope is that they may offer some stability and solid ground when it feels as if the earth is trembling beneath you.

I recommend using the audio recordings of these exercises, available at fierceboundaries.com, at least the first time you practice in this way. Once you have done these exercises a few times, you can try applying them informally, without guidance, at any time during your day, simply by pausing and gathering your attention on one single aspect of experience in the present moment.

Breath

The breath is with us from the moment we enter the world until the moment we depart our physical bodies. The signals that keep us breathing originate at the base of the brainstem and impact every aspect of our higher order functioning, from sensations and movement to emotions and even our thoughts and metacognition. As air flows into our lungs, they expand, and filter oxygen into the blood through the heart. As the heart pumps blood through the body, it sends this new oxygen to every cell, and gathers up what is no longer needed, the carbon dioxide, expelling this waste as the lungs contract. Each breath is an opportunity to start over, reset, and to let go of what is no longer useful. Many of us spend much of our lives unaware that we are breathing, without noticing the enduring rhythm and pulse of aliveness in our veins.

Every single person on earth is entitled to this life-giving breath, and even amid terror, pain, and extreme suffering, the breath stays with us, not judging our mistakes or discriminating because of skin color or size or age. The breath is inherently a present-moment experience. We cannot breathe a future breath or take back a past breath. And we don't often think about breaths we took or plan out breaths we should take tomorrow. There is only ever this breath happening right here, right now. It is also uniquely our own — we cannot breathe someone else's breath, and no one can breathe for us.

The breath is directly linked to our autonomic nervous system (ANS). When we are in sympathetic arousal (fight/flight), our breath becomes fast and shallow. When we are in parasympathetic mode (rest/digest), our breath slows and deepens. In fact, the relationship between the ANS and the breath is reciprocal — we can create states of anxiety and relaxation by speeding up or slowing down our breathing.

The breath is both voluntary and involuntary — it happens without us having to do anything at all, and at the same time we can breathe very much on purpose.

Awareness of breathing can be practiced at any time of day, regardless of how many tasks are on your to-do list, no matter where you are. Bringing the attention to a single breath can very quickly down-regulate our stress response, and bring our pre-frontal cortex back online, so that we can respond with more of our capacities available.

The following is an "Awareness of Breath" exercise that you can use to anchor attention. The first time you do this exercise, I encourage you to use the recording. Abbreviated instructions are provided below, and a 9-minute guided audio is available at fierceboundaries.com.

Exercise 3.1: Awareness of Breath

Start by adopting a posture that supports paying attention. You can close your eyes or simply rest your gaze a few feet in front of you.

Bring your attention to rest on the physical sensations of air entering and leaving the body. Notice the movement of the chest as the lungs expand and contract. Become aware of the rising and falling of the belly, or the movement of the ribs.

You might notice the temperature of air entering and leaving the nostrils, or the sensation of air hitting the back of the throat. It can be helpful to place a hand on the belly or the chest, or even just under the nose to support paying attention to the rhythm and movement of the breath.

After a few moments, you may notice that attention is pulled into thinking or planning, or sounds. This is completely normal. As best you can, simply notice that attention has shifted, and with kindness and non-judgment, gently redirect attention back to the sensations of breathing, again and again.

If it is challenging for you to feel the sensations of the breath or to sustain attention with the breath, ask yourself, **"how do I know that I am breathing?"** See if you can trace attention for the full length of a single breath, all the way from the beginning of the inhale to the completion of the exhale.

Give yourself time to study the breath, investigating with a spirit of kind, curiosity. Allow each moment of awareness of the breath to be a gift you are offering yourself, the opportunity to let yourself be worthy of your own attention, and to let just breathing be enough.

Reflection: What did you notice as you brought awareness to your breath? Are there opportunities throughout the day to breathe intentionally, or even to invite others to breathe with you?

Body

Those of us who deal with chronic stress and anxiety likely spend quite a bit a time living in our heads. When we are wrapped up in thoughts, we can easily forget that we even have a body. But fortunately for us, the body is always here, doing what it needs to do to survive and sending us information anyway, even if we are not always paying attention.

Physical literacy refers to having the capacity to sense into the body's knowing and translate the signals the body sends into information about what is needed. For example, a squeeze or pang in your stomach might indicate hunger, or dryness in your throat might signify thirst.

Awareness of physical sensations and the ability to discern what is needed and to respond to them is a foundational skill for managing stress and setting effective boundaries. This is especially true since our body sends us the first warning signals when we need to act in the interest of our physical and relational safety much sooner than our brains can process the chain of thoughts associated with whether we should act.

Our body operates on electrical signals. Like a supercomputer that is always sending and receiving information, the brain, heart, and autonomic nervous system make up our circuitry, and our conscious and subconscious mind and memories function as the operating system. Our electromagnetic field even extends outside of us three feet beyond our skin and detects subtle electrical cues from others in our environment. In this way, the body and mind are inseparable from each other, and some therapeutic modalities have even combined the two into a single word: the "**bodymind.**"

We are constantly receiving information from these electrical signals about what is happening inside of us (**interoception**), about the position of our body in space in reference to the world around us (**proprioception**), and from environmental stimuli, like visual and sound cues (**exteroception**).

Physical literacy can be strengthened through gentle mindful movement, yoga, massage, and body-based meditations. Even though many of us have not intentionally strengthened our physical literacy, this is an innate capacity that we all possess. All we need to do is be willing to *tune in* to the sensations in our bodies, rather than *tune out*.

Trauma, or overwhelming memories from our lived experience can influence how we relate and react to this sensory information. This can result in a separation from our bodies and poor physical literacy, and we might find that we don't know why we are reacting or feeling a certain way, or we might be plagued by chronic tension, prone to injury, or coping with our symptoms by using drugs or alcohol. It is normal for trauma survivors to feel disconnected from their felt experience, but the good news is that we can increase our ability to attend to sensations through regular practice and by asking for help. A skilled trauma therapist or mental health professional can guide you in this process if you need support. It's okay to take it slow, and to start with a part of the body that feels safe and manageable.

In the next exercise, we'll experiment with directing our attention to the sensations in our bodies, paying particular attention to posture. How we hold ourselves matters, and often the pain and constriction we feel in our bodies relates to chronic patterns of tensing, bracing, and holding that are deeply engrained in our subconscious awareness. Sitting in a position of dignity sends a message of worthiness to the bodymind, just as slumping in a posture of defeat sends a message of helplessness.

Giving yourself permission to intentionally practice sitting in a self-supporting and upright posture is an important step to reclaiming yourself and for embodying presence, attentional control, and self-worth. The following is an "Awareness of Physical Sensations" exercise that you can use to anchor attention. The first time you do this exercise, I encourage you to use the recording. Abbreviated instructions are provided below, and a 9-minute guided audio is available at fierceboundaries.com.

Exercise 3.2: Awareness of Physical Sensations

Start by feeling the sensations of your feet making contact with the floor and your body pressing into the chair or whatever surface you are sitting on.

Notice sensations of pressure, feeling gravity in the body. You are welcome to close your eyes, if it helps to notice sensations in the body, or just allow your eyes to rest on the ground a few feet in front of you in a half-open and receptive gaze.

Adopt a posture in your body that is self-supporting and upright.

Lengthen your spine, increasing the space between the vertebrae. Pull your back off of the chair slightly, maybe even scooting forward on the chair, so that your back is in a dignified posture, and you're not tempted to slump into your chair or collapse your shoulders.

Bring the shoulders up to the ears a few times and roll the shoulders so that they can settle. Breathe in as you bring the shoulders upward and breathe out as you drop the shoulders. As you release the shoulders, you might imagine you are taking off a heavy backpack, letting them know they don't have to carry anything right now.

Widen the attention to include the entire body sitting. You might notice that attention is pulled towards areas of tension in the body, or that you are distracted by hearing, thinking, or planning. When this happens, acknowledge that attention has shifted, and without judging yourself, gently guide attention back to the dignified posture of the body sitting.

As you practice sitting and paying attention in this way, you might become aware of some habitual patterns in the body. Perhaps there is a chronic curling in of the shoulders, or collapsing of the belly, or tightening of the jaw. When you notice these habits, you can gently direct some loving awareness towards them, breathing into these areas of tension, and bringing an attitude of kind curiosity to your experience.

When you are ready, you can transition out of this practice by inviting some movement back into the hands and legs and opening the eyes if they have been closed.

Reflection: What was it like to pay attention to sensations in the body while maintaining a self-supporting posture? What patterns of slumping, holding, bracing, or tensing did you notice?

Seeing

Within the landscape of seeing, we have endless choices for where we can place our attention. Where and how we fix our eyes in our environment influences how we experience what we are taking in and how we are perceived by others. Making good eye contact is something that can make others seem trustworthy, and shifty eyes that look away or to the left can signify evasiveness or lying. Avoiding eye contact can be a way to protect yourself during a conflict and staring directly at someone can be threatening or a way to assert dominance.

Our attention goes where our eyes go and our eyes are the windows to the world. When we start to cultivate attentional control and choose how and what we see, we can assert boundaries around what we are willing to look at, and the parts of us that we allow to be seen.

How we perceive and interpret what we see through our eyes can also be clouded by our life experience and negativity bias. We see what we want to see, or at the very least, what we are conditioned to see, and this narrowness or breadth of vision can have an impact on our thoughts, behaviors, emotions, and reactions. By slowing down and bringing awareness to our patterns of perception and seeing, and the automaticity of our interpretations, we can start to put more options on the map for reclaiming our attention.

The first time you practice the following Awareness of Seeing exercise, I encourage you to use the 5-minute audio recording available at fierceboundaries.com.

Exercise 3.3: Awareness of Seeing

Stand or sit outdoors or in front of a window where you can see a wide landscape in front of you. If you don't have a window available you can also do this practice indoors, looking at a wall across the room.

Start to bring your attention to the landscape of seeing. Notice the entire field as it appears in front of you through the eyes. Let your eyes explore what's here. You might start to notice colors, textures, movement or stillness, and shapes. Just allow yourself to take in what is here to be seen, bringing this spirit of inquiry and curiosity to the landscape of seeing.

Now, allow the attention to focus on a single object that appears in the landscape of seeing. You don't need to go out seeking the perfect object, just allow the gaze to fall upon one specific thing that you're seeing. With this single object of focus, again start to notice colors, textures, shape, and any movement or lack of movement.

Release the attention from this single object of focus and return the awareness to the larger landscape of seeing that appears before you. Widen the gaze and complete this practice when you are ready.

Reflection: What did you notice when you brought attention to the single object of focus? How was this way of paying attention different than focusing on the breath or sensations in the body? How might you apply this practice in moments of difficulty?

One of the things I love about this Awareness of Seeing exercise is that it helps me ground my attention with something that is *outside* of my body. Because my primary symptoms of post-traumatic stress are intrusive thoughts and chronic pain, paying attention *inwardly* is sometimes very difficult. I tend to become easily overwhelmed in the sea of explosive experiences happening in my emotional body and in my thoughts, and it can sometimes feel like heavy lifting to try to focus on my breath or sensations in my body.

I use this single tasking seeing practice all the time when I feel hijacked by challenging experiences and even have a favorite spot near my home where I like to stop on my daily walk with the dogs to do this. Here I can pause and look out at the wide view of the desert, sagebrush, mountains, and sky. Then I narrow my attention down to the tips of the grasses just in front of me and watch them glisten in the sunlight and dance in the wind. Then I widen my gaze again and continue my walk, feeling calmer and more centered with myself. No matter what turmoil I am facing, it gives me an increased sense of rest and peace every time.

Even in drab conference rooms or staring at the ceiling at the dentist office, where I am cut off from nature and there is little that feels nourishing to look at, this practice has offered me a sense of agency and refuge. I can always find something neutral within the landscape of seeing to bring curiosity to if I am intentional about it. Once, I even guided this practice for a group of students in a room where there weren't any windows, so they all gazed at a brick wall for five minutes. It was remarkable to hear their reflections afterwards, as so many of them found something truly interesting to explore when they focused their attention on a single area of the wall. They were astonished that something so apparently "boring" could become engaging, just by changing the way they were seeing.

Sound

Unwanted sounds can be a huge source of irritation when you are already stressed. But often, it is not the sound itself that causes us to be irritated, it is the relationship to the sound, and wanting it to be different that can really get to you. For example, you might be trying to finish a report or read the next juicy chapters of a book in a noisy household and find that you can't concentrate because the sounds keep distracting you. So, you go to a library or a coffee shop to get away, but then, you find that the intermittent sound of the espresso grinder, or the squeaking of the wheels on the library cart grates at you and disrupts your focus. So, you put on headphones and listen to music to drown out the noise and you're just starting to get going again when a loud talker sits down at the table next to you and proceeds to hold a boisterous conversation punctuated by bursts of raucous laughter.

Setting a boundary to create the conditions you want is difficult in this situation where you have little to no control of your surroundings or other people's behavior. You *could* make a dramatic frustrated gesture, heave an exasperated sigh, and tell the person next to you to "please shut the hell up," but that's not likely to go well for you, or to leave you feeling calm, regulated, and focused. You could also leave and try to find another place to work where there aren't sounds, but then you've lost time and energy, and you may not find a more suitable location anyway. Trying to simply "ignore" the sounds can also be quite challenging and it may seem like the more you try to drown them out, the louder they become. Resistance is futile, after all.

You can't fight it, you can't change it, but if your mental fitness is strong enough, you can notice that sound is present, then gently redirect and shift your attention with intention, and calmly place it where you want it. You can practice this skill with a brief attentional exercise. A recorded 6-minute version of this exercise using a mindfulness bell is available at fierceboundaries.com.

Exercise 3.4: Awareness of Sound

Start by adopting a posture that supports paying attention. You can close your eyes or simply rest your gaze a few feet in front of you.

When you are ready, bringing your attention to your ears, and allow yourself to receive sounds as they arise in your environment. There is no need to create any special conditions or silence anything around you, simply allow yourself to notice the sounds as they come and go.

Notice sounds that are close, and sounds that are farther away, or even notice sounds inside the body. Become aware of the tendency to label sounds, or wanting or not wanting sounds, and see if you can simply allow sounds to be as they are — sensations of the ears, arising and passing.

You might notice thoughts about sounds, or your relationship to sounds, and as best you can, return to the perspective of the observer, watching sounds come and go. You can even notice the space in between sounds, and the absence of sounds.

When you are ready, gently release sound as the object of attention and complete this practice with a full breath in and out and bring this moment-to-moment attention into the next moments of your day.

Reflection: What did you notice as you brought your attention to sound? How might you use this practice during your daily life?

Here's a story about awareness of sound: My very first mindfulness training was held in a large lecture hall in a university. We began our lessons on a Saturday when everything was quiet on campus and spent the weekend doing guided meditation practices with long stretches of time sitting in silence. At first, it was very challenging to stay focused on one thing. My thoughts jumped all over the place, and I had to redirect my attention to my breath again and again.

When the room got quieter, my thoughts got louder, like there were thousands of ping pong balls bouncing everywhere inside my head. The facilitators called it "monkey mind" and said it was normal. They reminded us that the purpose of mindfulness meditation is not to silence the mind or achieve an absence of thoughts, but to notice when attention shifted away from our intended focus and bring it back. When this happened, they encouraged us to use a soft mental note, such as *thinking,* and then to bring attention back to an anchor, without judging ourselves.

By 7:30 Monday morning, my attention had finally started to settle, and I found the silence between instructions was more spacious and nourishing than it had been on that first day. Then, 20 minutes into our morning meditation, the campus suddenly filled with people and the thin dividing walls between our room and the classroom next to us did little to block the noise. We could hear everything.

As the volume of the chatter ebbed and flowed, I noticed my thoughts grating at me. Even though silence had been uncomfortable at first, all I wanted now was peace and quiet, and my attention kept getting pulled into the little bits of conversation I could hear. I couldn't focus on myself with the teacher shouting math problems every few minutes and the students making so much *noise.* I got frustrated that our practice was getting interrupted in this way.

"Sounds are present," the facilitator said then, in a gentle, lilting voice. "See if you can allow them to be here, as they are part of the meditative field, but let them recede into the background."

Remarkably, what happened next was that I opened my awareness fully to the sounds coming and going, accepted that I could not change them, and realized that I could choose to focus on my breath instead, because *I was in control* of where I put my attention. All of the frustration vanished when I allowed the sounds to be a part of my experience and let go of attachment to things being different than they were.

The facilitator continued, saying, "you might even choose to celebrate these moments of noticing attention has shifted, as *this* is the practice of mindfulness."

In the years since that training, I have used this skill dozens of times when I have needed to reclaim my attention in a noisy environment. It's been helpful through constant construction noise on my rural street, it's given me agency when I'm bulldozed in conversations with my ex and offered me a diversion when I've been forced to sit through an unnecessary meeting led by someone who loves the sound of their own voice and over-explains everything.

Because I am a highly sensitive person, and I grew up in a noisy and chaotic household, sound can easily overstimulate me and trigger my anxiety. When I become aware that there is too much noise in my system, and that sounds are overwhelming me, I have found it incredibly helpful to apply this skill of letting sound recede into the background, acknowledging that it is unpleasant, then to choose another sensory experience to attend to. Sometimes I shift attention to sensations in my feet, or stand and stretch, but most often I use the anchor of my breathing. Intentionally shifting attention in this way gives me a sense of control over my experience and gives me some of my power back.

Skill: Shifting Attention with Intention

So far, we've practiced single tasking with four different internal and external anchors – breath, body sensations, seeing, and sound. The next step in reclaiming our attention is to purposefully lift our attention from one anchor and place it on another.

We've already done this briefly with the "Introductory Mindfulness Practice" from Chapter 1, and we'll continue to hone this skill throughout this book. It is perhaps the single most important skill you can have in your toolkit for regulating your nervous system, managing intrusive thoughts, and for setting boundaries that empower and protect you from engaging with the traumatized behaviors and attitudes of others.

Being able to release attention from where we are hooked, then ground attention with a different part of our present moment experience, gives us the opportunity to widen our awareness to the perspective of the observer and to be the witness of our own experience. It is from this place of wise knowing and all-encompassing loving presence that we can really start to put boundaries in place that are caring, kind, and in service of greater harmony and whole systems wellbeing.

For the following Object Meditation exercise, you can use any available object that can be held comfortably in the palm of your hand. If possible, I recommend an object that contains some quality of the natural world, such as a stone, flower, seashell, or pinecone. I hope this practice can be one that you carry with you, and I invite you to use it everywhere you go.

You are welcome to use the 5-minute audio recording available at fierceboundaries.com and feel free to share it with others. This is a great activity to share with kids of all ages and can help them reset their nervous systems and cultivate curiosity about the natural world.

Exercise 3.5: Object Meditation

Pick up an object that is available in your immediate environment. Bring attention to physical sensations. Notice the weight, texture, feel the contact of the object with the skin of the hands.

Engage the eyes. Become aware of the color, light and shadow, scratches or markings, shape. What is there to notice that you haven't seen before?

Bring the object to a nostril and notice any smell, or lack of smell. Try the other nostril and notice if there is any difference.

Bring the object to an ear and bring attention to any qualities of sound that are available. Try the other ear.

If the object is edible, take a small bite and really notice what happens in the mouth. If it is not edible, perhaps just bring it towards the lips, and notice any sensations that arise, or imagine what it might taste like.

Reflection: What is it like to bring attention to an object in this way? How might you use an object or this practice to help you stabilize attention in moments of difficulty?

Another interactive version of this exercise commonly used in trauma work that does not require a physical object is the **5, 4, 3, 2, 1 game**. The invitation is to name five things you see, four things you hear, three things you feel, two things you smell, and one thing you can taste. Again, this is a wonderful grounding and centering activity to offer to children to help them regulate amid difficulty.

When my daughter and I are in distress, trying to recover from an altercation with a classmate, a nightmare, or a scary situation, we do an abbreviated version by taking turns naming at least three things we see, hear, and feel. By the time we are done, both of us usually feel better, more grounded, and more connected with each other, and our attention is no longer hooked into what upset us.

Applied/Informal Attention Exercises

Single tasking, sensory awareness, and orienting practices can be incredibly effective for helping us reclaim our attention and regulate during moments of acute stress and crisis. While formal meditation is certainly beneficial, evidence is also emerging that these informal, in-the-moment and applied moments of attentional focus are effective interventions for trauma healing and long-term habit change. Data from clinical programs like MBSR and MBCT supports this evidence.

Participants in 8-week MBSR courses do an activity called the "raisin exercise" during the first session, in which they are given a single raisin, and directed to bring awareness to it through the senses, one sense at a time. After about five minutes of taking in all this sensory information, participants are invited to slowly place the raisin in the mouth and chew the raisin, then to swallow it and notice what it is like to be one raisin heavier.

When asked to reflect on this experience, participants overwhelmingly report that they are astonished at the burst of flavor they experience, and the enjoyment of a single raisin that is possible by slowing down and paying attention with their senses. Even those who claim not to like raisins often find that they experience a new level of appreciation for this tiny piece of dried fruit.

The takeaway is that slowing down and attending to the senses gives us the opportunity to savor our experience, and that there is richness and beauty in seemingly mundane activities when we are fully awake to them. A guided audio recording of the raisin exercise is available at fierceboundaries.com if you'd like to try it.

The more you practice attending to what you are doing while you are doing it, taking an intentional breath, or noticing what you are experiencing through the senses during times when you are not activated, the more you build neural pathways and train your mind to have access to this skill amid difficulty. With consistency and regular practice, you might even find that reclaiming your attention helps you live life more fully, welcome yourself home, and offers you new opportunities to belong in your body, and to love yourself, just as you are.

The following is a list of daily activities that you can bring mindfulness awareness to, simply by allowing yourself to "single task" and just focus your awareness on one thing.

Eating
Drinking a glass of water

Stretching
Sweeping the floor
Washing your hands
Doing the dishes
Doing laundry
Playing with your children
Petting the dog
Walking
Cleaning
Organizing
Reading a book
Dancing
Playing music
Listening to music
Gardening
Exercising
Taking a shower or bath
Making a to-do list
Grocery shopping
Cooking

Often our relationship to chores or mundane tasks is one of "doing mind," as a burden, or as something that needs to be completed to get to something better. Over the coming weeks, I challenge you to shift your perspective about these activities. Rather than perceiving them as something that needs to happen on the way to a bigger and better moment, see if you can allow yourself to be fully alive and present with them. See if you can change your relationship to the task from being something you "*have* to do" to one that you "*get* to do," and a chance to squeeze in a quick mental fitness workout.

In this way, every day activities can become opportunities for mastering your mind, building loving awareness, and giving yourself the gift of belonging right where you already are.

Chapter 4: You Are the Work

In the Fall of 2019, I got sick. At the time, I was the Executive Director of the Rocky Mountain Mindfulness Center, and I was single-handedly running the entire operation. This meant that I was responsible for website maintenance, event planning, fundraising, donor relations, tenant management, seeing individual clients for therapy, *and* the teaching of multiple MBSR and MBCT classes and weekend workshops. Meanwhile, my finances were a wreck, and I was still a single mother trying to make ends meet. My daughter was five years old and in kindergarten. To say I was overwhelmed and overloaded is a severe understatement.

When the unreasonable pace that I was trying to keep finally caught up with me, my body crashed, hard. I was confined to my bed with a fever, migraines, and severe joint pain, and my digestion went completely haywire. This resulted in rapid weight loss and the subsequent malnourishment gave way to brain fog and blurred vision exacerbated by screen usage. The slightest effort towards "getting work done" led to total mental fatigue to the point that I was not even capable of reading or responding to an email. Everything got put on hold, and because there was no one else in my organization to pick up the slack, my dozens of course participants and clients were left hanging, waiting for me to get better.

Doctors were unable to pin down a diagnosis and test after test came back negative. They told me that according to their results, I was perfectly healthy and suggested my illness might be "stress-related" or psychosomatic. They even praised me for losing weight. While mental effort instantly exhausted me, what I *was* able to do was take short hikes up into the mountains. Time in nature was the only thing that made me feel better.

On these hikes, I needed to rest frequently. So, I would find a soft place under a tree and lie down on the ground where I felt a deep physical relaxation. Sometimes, I even fell asleep. On the days that I took time for these forest naps, they re-energized me enough that I was even able to resume work for a couple hours. The guilt, however, was loud and intense. I felt like I was abandoning my responsibilities by taking time to hike in the woods, like I was letting everyone down by slipping away.

When I mentioned this to my therapist, she nodded knowingly and said, "you have to be nourished to be nourishing to others. It sounds like your time in nature is what you really need to heal yourself right now." She continued to explain to me that the time I was spending in the trees was time that my nervous system and my body needed to establish a new baseline of regulation and balance. She also said that perhaps when I returned to the office after soaking in nature, I was bringing that felt experience of the trees with me into my interactions with others.

"You get to bring the mountains to your clients because your nervous system speaks so much louder than your words. If you are exhausted and depleted, that's what your clients will get from you. But if you are resourced in a way that serves you, then you get to share that calm regulation with them because we are so contagious. *Your nervous system is the intervention. You are the work.* Do you think you can repeat that back to me?"

"My nervous system is the intervention. I am the work. *I* am the work? I *am* the work. Yeah, I guess I am." Relief washed over me as I recognized the truth in what she was telling me. There was no way I could sustain the level of output I had previously expected of myself, and trying to do so was a disservice to my clients and my daughter because look at where it had gotten me — so fatigued and burned out that my body and brain had completely revolted.

Eventually, I visited a naturopath who was able to diagnose me with mono and chronic Lyme disease and offer an effective treatment plan. This included a regimen of daily supplements in addition to a tincture that would kill the harmful bacteria, careful monitoring of what foods I ate (eliminating all gluten, sugar, and dairy, all of which exacerbated inflammation) and restraining myself from overcommitting my time and energy.

Recovery took several months, and I was not fully myself again until the global pandemic struck in 2020. In many ways, Covid-19 was a blessing to me because it gave me an exit strategy from a lifestyle that I could never return to, now that I recognized my limitations and had gotten real about how much pressure I put on myself. "I am the work," has become a mantra of sorts that gives me permission to care for myself in ways that may never be compatible with the fast-moving world of corporate America and education, and that's okay.

In the years since my diagnosis and recovery from Lyme, prioritizing my wellness and time in nature, and carefully choosing what foods I ingest and what commitments I make has been a game-changer. Being resourced and discerning in this way has allowed me to be available in a deeply healing capacity to people who hold entire systems in their circle of care, and to be the mom I've always wanted to be for my daughter.

I am deeply grateful to my illness for offering me the wisdom to know that self-care isn't selfish, but it is actually an act of service because it allows me to show up for others fully present, with all of my capacities online, and available to support them in setting their own fierce boundaries and making positive changes that really matter.

Your Nervous System is the Intervention

It's no secret that the majority of working adults are living in a state of chronic stress and anxiety. Many of us are under-resourced trauma survivors, living with normalized symptoms of post-traumatic stress. Our collective experience of this widespread mental dis-ease is a result of spending our lifetimes surrounded by traumatized nervous systems and triggering stimuli. We have been trained away from allowing ourselves to experience what we are feeling while we are feeling it, and to live in this zone of perpetual hyper-arousal and never-enoughness. The fear is very real, and it is easy to over-attend to high levels of threat and to negate the need for rest and regulation. Self-care is a radical act that requires us to be fierce in our commitment to disengaging from a culture of perpetual crisis.

Living in fear, reactivity, exhaustion, demoralization, and hyper-arousal is not sustainable, and even though so many people-pleasers have been taught to set our own needs and emotions aside, we simply cannot continue to do so without consequences. Medical doctor and researcher Gabor Mate[2] has proven that many terminal medical conditions and diagnoses are stress related. He claims that repressed feelings and unresolved trauma have been shown to be significant contributing factors for chronic pain, depression, suicidality, addiction, and even cancer. He even says that people-pleasers are the most likely to get sick, even when they eat well and exercise.

I understand that you are not likely to read these words and instantly stop wanting to make other people happy and immediately focus all your attention entirely on yourself. Caring for others is not the problem. The problem is failing to resource ourselves or to prioritize our own wellbeing and emotional needs before charging onto the battlefield of hearts and minds. You cannot run a marathon without fuel. You cannot work a double shift without pausing to take a few breaks. You cannot walk hundreds of miles through the desert without water. You must resource and nourish yourself to be a source of nourishment for others.

The following exercise will support you in connecting with your resources, grounding attention, and increasing your capacity to be a nourished presence for others. Abbreviated instructions are provided for this exercise below and a 13-minute guided audio of the full practice is available at fierceboundaries.com.

Exercise 4.1: Resourcing Practice

Adopt a comfortable and upright posture that is relaxed and engaged. Bring attention inward to the body sitting. Notice sensations of gravity and pressure in the body and let yourself settle. Choose an anchor and rest attention here for a few rounds of breath.

Bring to mind some experiences that are predictable, stabilizing, and rhythmic. This might be as simple as becoming aware of gravity, the beating of your heart, adopting a gentle sway side to side, or noticing the rhythm of the breath, coming and going. Or you might bring to mind a favorite song or piece of music, or any other external resource, such as a person or place that has some quality of safety, a pet, or the view of a tree or a mountain outside your window.

Notice any feelings of comfort or restfulness that arise as you attend to your chosen area of focus. What sensations do you notice in your body? As best you can, stay with this feeling for a few moments. Take some time to marinate here in the awareness of this resource. If it is challenging to keep attention with your resource, know that this movement of mind is completely normal. It's okay to stabilize attention with your anchor whenever you notice yourself getting distracted.

Complete this practice by naming the sensations that accompany the felt sense of safety or comfort in the body, letting this feeling make an imprint. Linger with this feeling for a few more rounds of breath, allowing yourself to fully absorb the felt sense of this resource, as best you can.

Reflection: What resource did you land on as an anchor? Can you describe the sensory details that accompanied this experience of safety? What do safety and comfort feel like in your body? Really give yourself permission to explore this so that you can return to this as a refuge during times of upheaval.

Co-Creating Safety in Systems

Many people first come to therapy, or classes like MBSR and MBCT in times of personal upheaval, or when they just can't take it anymore because their system is revolting like mine did. Perhaps they are experiencing panic attacks or navigating a tumultuous divorce. They may have sustained a physical injury, received a high blood pressure diagnosis, or they are under pressure at work or financial stress, and they can't sleep at night. Or they are caught in the spiral of adding more stress to their system with their substance use and reactivity and they have damaged relationships or reached a breaking point. When they begin these programs, they are easily knocked off balance, and they are desperate to reduce their stress and change their thinking patterns, so they can finally stop making it worse for themselves.

For these programs to be effective, the facilitator must be grounded and resourced. Our nervous systems are extremely sensitive to other's internal states, and we have evolved to be able to detect the electromagnetic fields of other people. Your ability to do this may be even more attuned if you were raised in an unpredictable household where you needed to be able to pick up on subtle cues that the environment was unsafe. We are inherently designed to be able to sense and feel each other, without the need for verbal communication and we have mirror neurons that synchronize us with the electromagnetic and non-verbal signals from each other. Our emotional states impact each other and the more regulated we are, the more we can be a source of regulation for others. This phenomenon is called **co-regulation**.

Many of you in caregiving, family, or organizational leadership roles may find that you are frequently in contact with people experiencing acute traumatic arousal, or chronic traumatic distress. Because of how contagious our nervous systems are to each other, it is critical to not only develop skills for managing our own arousal, but also to have the capacity to keep ourselves regulated amid the collective dysregulation that surrounds us. We need to be able to discern what emotional states are arising within our own nervous system and what does not belong to us so that we can stay grounded with our own experience and perhaps even offer our calm regulation to others.

Both our positive and negative moods can spread in a ripple effect through our communities, though research has shown that positive moods ripple outward more easily than negative ones[3]. We still need to take care that we are not allowing ourselves to become overwhelmed by a negative emotion because these mood-states do have a significant impact on our environment. For example, if we are under-rested, snippy, irritable, or anxious, the chances are higher that others may pick up on our moods and respond with defensiveness, tension, avoidance, or conflict. Perhaps you have noticed the change in the energy of a group when someone walks in the room in a state of high stress and anxiety. The air bristles with electricity, and everyone shifts in their seats uncomfortably, suddenly on guard and tense. If there are survivors of relational trauma in the room (which there most likely are) this may even send them into their own shame spiral or trigger them into reactivity.

One participant in a recent class, a woman named Ana, the director of Title IX at a state university, stated, "I work with a lot of people in trauma, and they just live in a really dark place." She had resigned herself to the fact that walking in the door to work meant leaving any joy and happiness at the door. Until participating in the mindfulness class, Ana had never considered that there might be a way to protect herself from soaking up the darkness and create safety for others by tending to herself first. "I work with people who are crying, and recounting terrible experiences, and we want so much to look away. But literally our job is not to look away. It's exhausting."

So how can we stabilize our attention with an anchor so that we can both tend to our own experience and be present for others without compromising our own wellbeing? This is truly a challenge in so many of our workplaces which are deeply relational and traumatized environments. To do this, we must commit and re-commit to resourcing ourselves fiercely, so that our own nervous system can serve as a port in the storm, without buckling. We also need a handful of concrete tools in our toolkit that we can draw on in these difficult moments.

As a reminder, we have already practiced this skill with the single tasking exercises in Chapter 3. By having this menu of objects on which we can place our attention in the present moment and using a variety of anchors, both internal (within the body) and external (outside of the body), we can deepen our capacity to be with what is arising without getting knocked off our center. Best of all, we can offer this stability to others simply by modeling the practice for ourselves. It can be as simple as asking others to take a breath with you. In working with educators for many years, I have witnessed many times how a calm, regulated teacher who is resourced and connected with their body can create a calm, regulated classroom, simply by doing what they need to do to care for themselves.

Additionally, we can bring collective awareness to our resourcing practice and establish community agreements in groups that set a tone of relational safety. Often, I work with the following three basic agreements:

- Take care of yourself and stay in choice. Honor your body's needs.
- Take care of each other and only share from your own, direct, present-moment experience.
- Come from nonjudgment, curiosity, and care.

These guidelines not only offer group members agency over their own experience, but also give them a sense of responsibility for the wellbeing of the group as a whole. Ironically, these agreements tend to have the most impact on students and staff members who are often labeled as "difficult" or "resistant." I believe that this shift happens because many of the "problem-children" in schools have been systematically stripped of their sense of agency and have been disempowered and prevented from honoring their body wisdom. Given the choice to not participate or do something differently with their body than everyone else puts them in the driver's seat of their own experience, often for the first time in their lives. When they do not get in trouble for being unique, this creates an environment where it is safe for them to be authentic. Empowering others to stay in choice with their attention and honor their knowing is sometimes the only act of defiance available to us in an authoritarian system that demands we abandon ourselves to succeed.

By the end of the 2-hour mindfulness session that day, our participant, Ana, had experimented with several different ways to reclaim her attention and find refuge in the present moment, helping her step out of habitual cycles of thought that previously made her too overwhelmed to be a resource for others. She left the class with renewed optimism and a sense of possibility for co-creating safety with those who needed her most.

Grounding Yourself in the Face of Extreme Distress

Recently, I attended a talk presented by Roshi Joan Halifax, a Buddhist teacher, Zen priest, and anthropologist, who told a story about being in Simikot, Nepal, where she was working in a medical clinic. She encountered many gravely injured children, and her role was to be the calm presence in the room.

She talks about one young girl with terribly infected burns, hearing the endless sharp cries of the child as the nurses cleaned her wounds, with no anesthetic. In attending to the child, Halifax had to continually monitor her own nervous system, and soon became overwhelmed by feelings of the child's and father's distress. In her book, *Standing at the Edge: Finding Freedom Where Fear and Courage Meet*, she describes coming very close to fainting and knowing that this would not be helpful to the child or nurses. As soon as she realized this, she immediately stepped back from the situation, so that she could resource herself:

"I realized that getting through this was not a matter of avoiding what I was witnessing; it was not a matter of shutting down, or walking out of the room, or letting go into a dead faint. I recognized that my identification with the child's experience had spiraled out of control, and if I were to stay in the room, I needed to shift from hyper-attunement to care, from empathy to compassion."

Halifax calls this condition "empathic distress," a form of vicarious trauma that arises from over-identifying with the suffering of another. It's likely that if you are a people-pleaser, peacemaker, caregiver, therapist, empath, or simply someone who cares and is working within a trauma-impacted system, you have experienced this phenomenon as well.

As tempting as it can sometimes be to run away in the face of extreme distress, it doesn't help anybody if we just say, "that's terrible, I'm out of here. Someone else can deal with it." Unfortunately, there are so many people in the world who do exactly this because we are not resourced enough to do anything other than lock up, numb, dissociate, and run away. This is one of the reasons we are so chronically dysregulated on a systemic level, and why we do not have skills for stabilizing ourselves first so that we can be with the discomfort of another without becoming overwhelmed.

I invite you to pause for a moment here and remember why you care. What was it that encouraged you to embark upon a caring and healing pathway in the first place? My guess is that your answer has something to do with love, which is a universal human experience. Keep this reason close to your heart and remind yourself of your purpose and intention often, because the world is full of suffering and when we are tired and blinded by moral outrage, it can be all too easy to forget why we do what we do. Unfortunately, those of us willing to do deep inner work and transform ourselves to keep our hearts available and of service to the greater good are still in the minority. But our numbers are growing. We have to keep going, but we have to do so in a regulated and boundaried way if we are going to survive.

How can we remain grounded when we are in the presence of something that is overwhelming or re-traumatizing for us to witness? How can we stay, like Roshi Joan Halifax did, by the side of that burned little girl, and care for ourselves without turning away?

Noticing that she was slipping into empathic distress and that her nervous system was overwhelmed, offered Halifax the opportunity to apply a grounding skill she had practiced many times.

"Catching myself in this fraught and fragile moment, I took a mindful in-breath and shifted my attention to my feet, to the simple sensation of the pressure of my feet on the floor. I gave myself a few seconds to get grounded. Then I recalled briefly that I was there to serve, as were all who were working with the child. I kept my awareness on my body and stayed firmly rooted to the earth. When my heart rate shifted and my vision began to clear, I lent my attention again to Dolma, and I could sense how resilient this little one was. All of this occurred in a matter of a minute or so."

As Halifax continued to share her story, she said, "I choose to bear witness to suffering without turning away."

As someone who has often felt like my emotions are too much for others to handle, this statement landed deep in my heart, and tears began to roll down my face as she spoke. There have been so many times in my life when I have been left alone in my suffering and longed for the companionship of someone willing to be with me in it, without turning away. I am a person with big feelings and expressing myself authentically seems to scare people and deter intimacy. Now, as a therapist, I understand the healing power of witnessing and holding space for another person's pain, and I have had to prioritize my own regulation so that I could be a source of stability for others. It takes consistent work and fierce dedication to my wellbeing. As soon as I stop caring for myself my capacity for holding space for others suffers and their pain becomes too much for me to carry.

I have often found myself wishing the system were set up in such a way that we didn't all have so much repressed distress, and that presence in the face of difficulty wasn't a monetized service that required special training. I wish embodied presence and skillful coping were taught in school, and that we all had capacity to bear witness to suffering without turning away. Despite my burnout as an educator and school leadership consultant, I still have hope that this shift is possible within a generation if we start to prioritize mental fitness at the decision-making level and support widespread wellness education from the top down *and* the bottom up. I have my fingers crossed that those of you reading this book who are willing to model these practices might also make a small dent in achieving this monumental task.

The following exercise offers a starting point that you can return to anytime, anywhere to help you ground and stabilize attention in moments of crisis, overwhelm, and suffering. It involves shifting attention out of your head, and down into the soles of your feet, the way Halifax did in her moment of empathic distress.

Exercise 4.2: Grounding Your Feet

If you're able, I invite you to come into a standing posture and to focus on the sensations of pressure as your feet touch the ground. You can do this with or without shoes, and if you need to stay seated, simply bring your feet down to the floor and notice the sensations of contact with the ground.

Feel gravity in the feet and start to explore the sensations of contact by rocking around on the four corners of the feet. You might start to sway or rock back and forth or come up onto your tiptoes and rock back onto

---

your heals. Notice how the movement of your body is experienced through the soles of your feet.

When attention is pulled into thinking or planning, simply note this movement of mind, and redirect your attention back to the sensations of your feet connecting with the earth beneath you.

If it feels available, you can bring an image of roots into your feet, imagining that as you feel down into the ground beneath you, you are sending roots into the earth that can stabilize you. Invite this sensation of rootedness to spread up into your legs, torso, arms, and shoulders, all the way up to the crown of your head.

With each inhale, lengthen your spine and with each exhale, drop your attention down into the bottoms of your feet, making a little more space for yourself to be just as you are, with each breath.

Reflection: What are you doing to resource yourself in response to suffering/stress that is already working? What strengths do you have that come from a place of your own resource/regulation? How do you know when you are becoming overwhelmed by the distress of another?

Moving Forward with Intention

I want to take a moment to pause and thank you for your willingness to come this far. If you are still reading, it is likely that transformation is already happening in your life, and you are being the change the world needs. It takes courage and dedication to walk this path, and the work you have put in deserves recognition and appreciation. With each step we take towards living with awareness and care, we are planting seeds of mental health, skillful coping, and kindness for future generations.

Check in with yourself and take a moment to consider whether it would be supportive to revisit any of the practices in these chapters before moving forward. Remember, the pathway of healing is not linear, and there is no destination. There is only this moment and our relationship to being with what's here, now. Continue to revisit the basic practices of grounding and orienting as much as you need to, and whenever you can, pause and ask yourself those two fundamental questions: What's here, and how can I best attend to what is arising?

The attitudinal foundations of the practices we have explored so far invite us to create safe resting places for ourselves in the present moment, to turn towards our pain, and to bring investigation and curiosity to our experience, so that we can care for ourselves *before we fall apart*. Each time we slow down and turn toward our experience, and allow ourselves to feel what we feel, we put new possibilities on the map for embracing our wounded-ness, welcoming our humanness, and improving our wellbeing. This is where deep healing begins. The more we can do this for ourselves, the more we can be the change we wish to see on a whole-systems level.

Chapter 5: Savor the Good

One of my favorite movies of all time is *Apollo 13*[5], the true story of the doomed 1970 space mission and miraculous rescue of astronauts Jim Lovell, Fred Haise, and Jack Swigert. I love this film partially for the storytelling and suspense, but mostly because this tension is created at the edge where looming disaster meets the NASA engineers' capacity to stay calm and focused during extreme crisis. It is a real-world example of applied mindfulness, skillful leadership, and mental fitness in action, demonstrating how paying attention and staying grounded when it is needed can save lives and that succumbing to fear and panic has deadly consequences.

In a climactic moment and turning point right after the catastrophic explosion, the crew discovers they are venting oxygen. There is a long pause, as the news of this inevitable death sentence sinks in, followed by CAPCOM 1 finally responding with "Roger, Odyssey, we copy your venting."

Then the room erupts into the chaos of acute crisis, frenzied activity, and worst-case scenarios. The engineers explode into action like Smurfs running from Gargamel, almost certainly overloading their systems with adrenaline and cortisol, and sending their PFCs offline. Jon Kabat-Zinn calls this tendency "catastrophizing[6]," and it is a normal, conditioned response to living in a landscape of perpetual crisis. Remember, our innate negativity bias causes attention to leap immediately to a perceived threat, and the dangers and potential bad outcomes of a situation, so the NASA engineers' response is understandable.

In response to the chaos, Gene Kranz, played by actor Ed Harris, pauses for a moment, quickly surveys the chaos, and says, "let's work the problem, people, let's not make things worse by guessing." To keep the ground staff and the astronauts from panicking, Kranz keeps himself calm and models single tasking, dealing with only one thing at a time. He is a beacon of regulation and clear, focused attention, operating with all of his capacities fully engaged. His team needs his stability and for his pre-frontal cortex to be working. The focus soon lands on the immediacy of the biggest problem — the inevitable disaster that faces the crew as they run out of oxygen. The ship is bleeding to death.

Now, I don't know if the real Gene Kranz had specifically trained his nervous system for a scenario like this one, but in the film, he demonstrates remarkable leadership skills by slowing down enough to avoid catastrophic thinking in this moment of extreme crisis. He pauses again, commanding attention in the room, takes a breath, and says, "Let's look at this from a standpoint of status … *What have we got on the spacecraft that's good?*"

This is a turning point in the crisis because this question instantly flips the script on the disaster narrative. The focus is immediately redirected toward what is possible, rather than over-attending to the problems and perseverating on the tragic possibilities.

Asking what on the injured spacecraft "is good" also puts the brakes on the collective fight/flight response in the room. It instantly changes the narrative, invites everyone to slow down, and makes the technician scrunch his eyebrows in concentration (thus bringing his PFC back online). The technician takes a sweaty breath and responds with, "I'll have to get back to you on that, Gene."

After a short period of investigation along this new line of inquiry, a plan begins to form. The collective mindset is now solution-focused and hopeful. Rather than lingering in the devastation of having "lost the moon," the only thing that matters now is to stop the "bleeding" as quickly as possible, and to save what's left so they can get the crew home alive. The recommendation is made to shut down the leaking fuel cells to try to save the remaining oxygen.

Once the loss of oxygen has been addressed, then the focus shifts to the journey home, using creative thinking, and by gathering all the limited resources the crew on board the spacecraft still has. By tackling one solution at a time, the astronauts finally arrive home safely, despite their harrowing re-entry. This is skillful leadership and crisis management at its very finest.

This NASA level of attentional training is what we need more of in this traumatized world of never-ending crisis. In our own lives as parents and leaders, we not only have the responsibility of captaining our own ships through severe weather and steering everyone to safety, but we must also be a beacon of calm and hope in the storm for our children.

We can level-up by flipping the script, just like Gene Krantz did at Cape Canaveral, and bring the focus of attention to what is working, rather than what's not. With the skills of resourcing and attentional control, we can be as effective as NASA engineers by staying calm, resourced, focusing on the task immediately ahead of us, and asking, "what have we got on the spacecraft that's good?"

The following reflection questions are derived from a framework called "Appreciative Inquiry."[7] In many ways, this is the very opposite of a "problem solving" approach. Appreciative Inquiry uses the strengths of a system to support visioning what is possible, rather than focusing on what is wrong and what needs to be fixed.

Take your time with this. You might even decide to do some abbreviated version of this activity each day, even if it is just a mental note or non-verbal acknowledgement.

Exercise 5.1: Resourcing through Appreciative Inquiry

- What is *already working within your family or professional system*? What successes and strengths can you identify that are already in place?
- See if you can recall what originally drew you to your current parenting/leadership/helping professional role. What is the most important thing that your work has contributed to your life?
- How does your intention and care result in positive outcomes for your staff/clients/patients/children?
- When you are feeling best about your work, what do you value about the task itself?
- Imagine you fall into a deep sleep and slept for 10 years. While you are sleeping, magical changes take place in your system. When you wake up, it is in an environment where your soul feels nourished, and you are fully resourced, and supported. Everyone's needs are being met, and your community is thriving and deeply connected. What specific changes do you see as you look around you?

Reclaiming Joy: Gratitude

Our modern world encourages us to rush all the time. There are so many lost opportunities for presence, connection, savoring what is pleasant, and practicing gratitude. It often takes a life-threatening experience or a devastating loss to wake people up to what they are missing. I hope that the content in this chapter so far have already given you the opportunity to pause and bring awareness to what is already working in your life, and to what is good enough.

Giving ourselves permission to savor the present moment, and to be joyful in a world that is full of so much pain and suffering, is indeed a radical act. Remember, *you are the work.* It is a completely worthwhile use of your time to bring attention to what's good and what is already working in your system. It may feel selfish, or you may notice guilt if you allow yourself to be happy when others around you are not. You may even have a sense of "foreboding joy," a feeling of "this is too good to be true," that you don't deserve to be happy, or that experiencing happiness is dangerous, because surely disaster is right around the corner.

But when we go through our whole lives expecting the worst to happen, this can have a long-term impact on our nervous system. Not only do we miss opportunities for joy, but in limiting ourselves from experiencing pleasure we often increase our distress. Whether you believe it or not, you deserve to experience happiness. Start small, with little moments of pleasure, such as the feeling of sunshine on your skin, the soothing scent of a cup of tea, the beauty of a flower, or any other mini moment of goodness.

Remember, your happiness ripples outward and impacts people around you, so by giving yourself permission to marinate in the green zone and savor your pleasant experiences, you can make the world a better place. The following gratitude exercise will support you in cultivating awareness of pleasant experiences. The first time you do this exercise, I recommend listening to the 14-minute guided audio available at fierceboundaries.com. Abbreviated instructions are provided here.

Exercise 5.2: Gratitude Practice

Adopt a comfortable and upright posture and bring attention to the body sitting. Focus attention on the feeling of gravity in the body and any sensations of pressure where the body makes contact with the floor or the chair.

Bring to mind some **simple pleasures** in life, perhaps a compliment or kindness that someone offered you recently, your favorite coffee mug, or the comfort of sunlight on your skin. Maybe you can recall the sound of the wind rustling in the trees, a trickling creek, or birds singing. Or perhaps, simply appreciate the ability to pause, to take a break, and to practice gratitude.

How does focusing on simple pleasures impact the way you are feeling in your body, in your mind, and in your heart?

Gently shift attention now and think of the **people who support you behind the scenes**. These might be people you don't often think about, such as delivery drivers, restaurant workers, and people who make medical supplies. See if you can tap into gratitude for their efforts and for what they do.

You might choose to place a **hand on your heart** as you invite thankfulness and gratitude, giving yourself permission to savor the moment. Notice if it's easy for you to tap into gratitude as you think of these things, knowing that there isn't a right or wrong way to feel right now. So whatever experience you are having, it's quite okay. It's all good information.

Now, see if you can bring your awareness to one **supportive person** in particular, someone who comes to mind right away. Try to think of them smiling, greeting you, and perhaps even imagine yourself saying thank you to them. This practice isn't about visualizing this person exactly, just getting a sense for how it feels to bring a quality of thankfulness to them.

Now we'll release this person from our attention and bring awareness to **yourself**. Often, it's quite difficult to be grateful to ourselves, because we tend to pick on the things we do wrong or the things that are challenging about ourselves. See if you can allow yourself a bit of kindness and curiosity as you think of your body and all it does for you, even when it's ill, even when it's hurt. Think of all the qualities that you admire about yourself, the work that you do, the time that you are taking now to do this practice. Pick one thing that you are thankful for about yourself, about who you are, a personality trait, or something that you do rather well. As best you can, rest in this feeling of gratitude for yourself, and perhaps offer yourself a "thank you." Thank yourself for all you do. Thank yourself for doing the best you can with what you have.

Complete by taking a deep breath into your belly, and perhaps letting it out with a sigh, inviting a bit of movement into your body, wiggling your toes and your fingers, swaying from side to side, and blinking your eyes open.

Reflection: What was it like to practice gratitude in this way? What was challenging? What was easy? How can you expand your gratitude practice into the next moments of your day? What would it look like to share your gratitude with others?

Look for the Helpers

Staying positive in a traumatized world can be challenging. Many of us who are helping professionals or parents trying to guide our children safely through their school years find ourselves surrounded by trauma everywhere. Even if we practice radical self-care and do all we can to stay resourced, we may still find ourselves cranky, bitter, and exhausted at the end of the day. It makes sense that you feel this way. I do too sometimes. The world is a mess.

Over time this vicarious trauma, chronic worry, and over-exposure to suffering can build up in our system and lead to burnout, compassion fatigue, and demoralization. Once we reach these depressive mind states, it can be very difficult to pull ourselves out of the hopelessness and despair. We can become locked into focusing on the pain and horror in the world and feel as if we do not have the strength to do anything to help, so why bother?

Demoralization happens when we are unable to do the good work we signed up to do. I've seen this happen frequently for educators and administrators who came into the field of education because they wanted to serve, teach, and have a positive influence on children. But the educational system has become so bogged down in standards, bureaucracy, and testing that there is no longer space for individuation and care. It is very frustrating to be an educator who understands the needs of their students but does not have the time, energy, or support to meet those needs. Worst of all, it's common for students who do seek support to end up harmed by the very systems that are meant to help them. It's confusing for them and heartbreaking for their teachers. All we want to do is help, and every effort fails. So, it makes sense that eventually we stop trying.

This "why bother" mindset is the attitude so many young people are growing up with in this age of unimaginable gun violence and uncertainty around climate change. The problems are too big for one person to address. The system is too broken for one person to make a difference. The planet is hurting, and nothing I do will help. My grandchildren may not even have water to drink or air to breath, so maybe we shouldn't have children at all. It's too painful to pay attention and it's useless to try to do anything to stop it, so might as well just quit while I'm ahead.

These are thoughts, not facts. They are the voices of fear-mongering media and depression speaking, and even though the neural pathways that drive these thoughts are strong, you don't have to listen to them. You can reclaim your thoughts and shift the focus of your attention to what is beautiful in the world. You can spend intentional time proactively attending to the small differences you *can* make, just by being the goodness you wish to see.

Energy follows thought, and if we continue to sink into apathy and overwhelm, little will be done to make positive changes that lead to the thriving and wellbeing of humanity. However, if we can find a glimmer of hope in the darkness and latch onto that instead, then we may just find our way to a brighter dawn.

Resilience and hope are the most important qualities that we can cultivate for ourselves and teach our children. Do not allow yourself to get sucked into the vortex of doom scrolling and catastrophic thinking. This is an area where fierce boundaries around what you attend to make all the difference, not just for your own personal happiness and wellbeing, but for future generations. We can teach our children to hope and believe that healing and a bright healthy future are possible.

The antidote to demoralization is to shift the focus of your attention to *where the good work is already happening*. In the same way, the antidote to burnout is to bring awareness to small moments of pleasure and activities that give you a sense of mastery. I invite you to start to notice small moments of goodness and efficacy everywhere you go. Just like cultivating a gratitude practice, you can start to habituate your mind to notice the acts of kindness that you see around you and the small ways you have a positive impact on the world.

If you can't find any goodness or acts of kindness happening, either look a little harder, or create them for yourself. Even a simple smile can go a long way towards brightening someone's day. Here's one moment of goodness from my life that gave me hope when I needed it:

A Moment of Goodness

I was in mid-sentence when I saw the old woman slip and fall out of the corner of my eye. She slid softly and silently down the steps, her body crumpling into the pool. She bobbed gently with her face in the water, her curled back lifting above the surface, her limbs unmoving.

I moved toward her, ready to act, without thinking about whether I should or not. A man nearby pushed through the water and reached her just before I did. He turned her body and gently lifted her head from the water. "Call 911" he said to me as I pulled my phone from my pocket and dialed. "Wait," he said, as she coughed and opened her eyes. "She's alright. Tell the front desk." I cancelled the call, and he propped her up on the step.

As I turned towards the reception area, I saw that the room around us had fallen quiet. Everyone was standing still, holding their breath, watching the scene unfold, with their bodies poised for action. Gentle looks of concern and care filled every face. How can I help? they all seemed to say.

I made it to the front desk quickly and interrupted a customer, saying firmly "a woman just passed out by the hot pool and fell in." There was an immediate response as multiple employees jumped into action. They were beside her, with first aid kits and juice before I could even turn around.

As I watched them tend to her, a surge of love filled my heart. The scene before me was calm, quiet, and controlled as they gathered around her and checked her vital signs.

All around me, I felt the electricity of human hearts throbbing with concern. The care in the air was palpable. For just a moment we were all here, together. These 45 seconds had stopped time and held us in an eternal moment of human heart connection.

"I almost drowned!" I heard the woman say, with an astonished giggle. She had the bright smile of someone who was suddenly delighted to be alive. She was going to live to love another day. Her family members arrived from the other end of the pool and gathered around her, wide-eyed and stricken with care.

One at a time, people began to exhale, and to return to their cheeseburgers and conversations. Trickles of relieved laughter filled the air. I felt my body start to relax, and the moment was over.

For the rest of the afternoon, the old woman was in my thoughts, and I was overcome by surges of gratitude and emotion around our innate and instinctual capacity to care for each other in times of need.

My response when I saw her fall was totally automatic, just like with the man who pulled her out of the water. There was no question of what we "should" do in that moment. Our brainstem reacted before we had time to process a cognitive thought or make a decision. We just acted.

It's moments of goodness like this that make me believe that humans are inherently good. We help because it is instinct. Survival is in our human nature, and so is belonging. At our core, we are designed to catch each other when we slip and fall face down into the pool. We are designed to care.

In the face of fear however, we can easily forget this universal bond that connects us all. We know from history and from generations of perpetuated trauma that we can be scared and numbed out of our care for each other — that we can even be trained to cause harm. But all you have to do is look into the eyes of a military veteran who has seen combat to know that this comes with a heavy price — deep moral injury, heartbreak, exile that can last generations, and karmic wounding that isn't easily vanquished.

When we carry generations of trauma and harm in our bodies and hearts, it can be so easy to believe that we are better off alone, or that no one would notice if we just disappeared, or that we shouldn't burden anyone with our needs. But there is no escaping that we are a social species, that we are designed for belonging, to live in community, and to be in relationship with other humans. Even though we are living in uncertain times, depression and addiction are rampant, and the future of the planet is at stake, I have hope, and I am reminded of our essential human goodness every day. It is important to remember this element of the human condition — that there is safety in numbers, that our hearts are meant for each other, and that we automatically leap into the deep end to save someone who is drowning.

I am so grateful to live in a time and in a place where we don't question whether or not to save a life, we just do it. Isn't this a reason to believe we are making progress as a human community? Isn't this a reason to have hope for the future?

Because from what I saw at the pool that day, our essence is good, and our intentions are pure when they are put to the test.

We can survive these times by acknowledging our interconnectedness and that we need each other. And we can take solace in our basic human instinct to lift each other to the surface, in our shared human experience of wanting each other to survive.

Reflection: Recall a moment of goodness that you witnessed, participated in, or received. How did it feel to help or receive help when it mattered? What do you notice in your body and heart as you recall this experience?

Savoring the Pleasant

Scientists have proven that intentionally nurturing positive states and practices like gratitude, loving-kindness, and focused attention can change the brain. They have even documented a decreased startle response among experienced meditators. Not only that, but evidence also shows that our emotional states are contagious, and that we can spread happiness even farther than we can spread fear and anxiety, and that by cultivating positive emotional states, we can improve the lives of people around us up to three times removed.

Each time we actively shift our perspective and cultivate positive mind states, we build new neural pathways and set a boundary for ourselves that says we refuse to be hijacked by a world in perpetual crisis.

We can also actively apply our understanding of negativity bias and neuroplasticity in the face of difficulty by bringing attention to the opposite of the distress that we are experiencing. For example, if everything feels uncertain and you're struggling with doubt, the practice can be to bring attention to what *is* certain (for example gravity, the breath, nature, and the predictability of the seasons). When workplace dynamics or the news feels heavy and serious, make some time for lighthearted play, connection, or a fun activity that you enjoy. If life feels out of balance or you feel wobbly and unstable, bring attention to what is rhythmic or ground attention down into a solid and stable posture in your body. Maybe even spend a few moments stacking and balancing some rocks or building a house of cards. If you're out running errands and it seems like everyone is stressed, anxious, aggressive, or unkind, pause. Spend a minute connecting inwardly and offer some kindness to yourself. Then look for the helpers and for little moments of kindness.

I promise they will be there when you are willing to bring attention to them because people are inherently good and filled with love for each other. When you find them, savor them, and let them linger in your awareness. So often, we rush through our moments of pleasure without fully enjoying them, and we don't give ourselves an opportunity to savor moments of goodness. In the following exercise, I invite you to bring awareness to the experience of savoring and see if you can give yourself a few extra moments to linger with these good feelings.

Abbreviated instructions are provided below to help you formally practice savoring. Remember, this is a new way of paying attention for many of us, so if this practice feels awkward or strange at first, know that this is completely normal. I recommend listening to the 9-minute guided audio available at fierceboundaries.com.

Exercise 5.3: Savoring Practice

Adopt a comfortable seated posture and bring attention inward to the body sitting. Take a few full rounds of breath, letting your system settle, and bring awareness to gravity in the body.

Now, shift attention towards any **pleasant sensations** in your body and invite a soft smile as you notice them. Are there areas that feel relaxed or at ease? If it's challenging to notice anything pleasant in your body, this is completely normal. Start by just noticing what is neutral, or perhaps there is some part of the body that is free from pain. You might also find it supportive to offer yourself some soothing contact or a gentle caress, perhaps rubbing your arm, or cradling your face in your hands. Smile to yourself, savoring these sensations of pleasure. See if you can stay with these pleasant sensations for a few moments, resting in the experience. It's okay to linger with the good feeling.

Now, I invite you to release attention from sensations in the body and bring to mind **a memory, person, or object that brings you a feeling of pleasure**. This might be remembering time spent with friends, or the smell of a loved one's sweater, the feeling of their arms wrapped around you, a place in nature, or even just remembering the texture of a favorite blanket, or the taste of your favorite food. Let this pleasant experience come to life in your sensory awareness and give yourself permission to savor it. Notice any sensations that arise in your body as you rest into the pleasure of this experience.

If it's too challenging to get in touch with pleasure, see if you can just become aware of **what is already working in the system**, without needing to put effort in to making it happen. The breath is coming and going. New oxygen is flowing into your cells and the body is releasing what is no longer needed. Gravity is keeping you firmly rooted to the ground. The earth is holding you.

See if you can notice any amount of relief or softening that happens as you give your weight to the earth and let yourself be held a little more. Rest into this softening and linger here for just a moment longer.

Reflection: What is it like to shift attention away from difficulty and savor pleasant or neutral experiences? How did it feel to offer these kind words to yourself? What would it look like to invite moments of savoring and noticing moments of pleasure into your daily life?

Beyond Gratitude Practice

Research shows us that naming three things we are grateful for each day can make us happier. However, if we list the same things over and over, we can actually find ourselves getting bored of gratitude practice, and it can even start to have negative effects. Below are some suggestions for expanding your gratitude practice to keep it interesting and to include others. The invitation is to bring some creativity and playfulness to how you practice gratitude. Feel free to add to the list.

- Name things about your body you appreciate.
- Take time to savor a few bites of your favorite food.
- Name processes/objects in nature that keep you alive.
- Play gratitude "I spy." *I spy with my little eye, something I'm grateful for that is purple…*
- Name things about your family/friends that bring you joy.
- Take a moment to send gratitude towards your modes of transportation, each time you make it somewhere safely.
- Name things about your office/classroom that support you in accomplishing your work.
- Name qualities of yourself that you enjoy sharing with others.
- Make a thank you note for someone who helped you.
- Practice random acts of kindness, without expecting recognition.
- **"Glimmer" Journal:** For the next week or more, I invite you to document the moments of goodness you witness, record your gratitude practice, or document moments of pleasure using a journal or notebook. Record the experience, what you noticed in your body, and what moods, thoughts, and feelings arose as you reflected. It's okay if you miss a day. When you remember, be gentle with yourself, and pick up where you left off, without judgment.

Chapter 6: Honor the Body You Have

Your body is the most clearly defined boundary you have, and it is one you should guard more fiercely than any other. Your skin separates you from the rest of the world, you belong inside it, and no one has the right to cross that boundary unless you invite them in. You were born here, and you will die here, and this body will be your vessel all the way. You must protect it and care for it as if it is a precious child, worthy of your attention and love.

Sadly, many of us have become estranged from our bodies, or experienced boundary violations such as sexual violence, forced manual labor, invasive medical trauma, body shaming, or physical attack. Some of you may even feel as if your body has betrayed you. I know that I did when my back gave out and I could no longer carry my three-year-old daughter without collapsing in blinding pain. But pain is the body's way of crying out for help, and healing this relationship is possible, if we're willing to listen.

Feeling at home in your body is complicated, and the journey to belonging begins long before we are even conceived. Baby girls are born with all their eggs already fully formed in their ovaries, which means that when your mother was born, the egg that would someday become you was already inside her. In some ways, the experience of your being human could even be traced back to your mother's conception, and your grandmother's pregnancy — the grandmother who was born with your mother's egg in her body, and so on back to the beginning of time.

The scientific evidence of how our nervous system, sense of belonging, and mental health are impacted by our experience in the womb continues to grow, and we now know that trauma experienced by our mother during her pregnancy can have long term effects. If a mother's pregnancy is calm, healthy, and characterized by a stable heart rate and a minimal exposure to adrenaline and cortisol (stress chemicals), the nervous system gets to develop in an environment that is predictable and **rhythmic**. Babies who are lucky enough to be born into these environments are more likely to have good mental health, lower risk for addiction and illness, and more resilience. In addition, their fear response system has been created in an environment of safety and their first experience of the world is more likely one of belonging and being welcomed.

The brainstem is the first part of the nervous system to develop when we are forming, and this is the part of the brain responsible for our basic human functions – heartbeat, blood pressure, breathing, hearing, swallowing, balance, and facial sensations. These are also the functions most closely tied with our threat detection system and the autonomic nervous system.

Therefore, if a pregnant mother is not getting her basic needs met, or if she is exposed to violence, high levels of stress, or unpredictable frightening behavior, the growing fetus receives **arhythmic** input and sudden blasts of fear chemicals. Babies born in this situation (which is many of us) tend to startle easily, to be primed for high levels of stress reactivity, and to be prone to anxiety, depression, and addiction. These children are born with a nervous system that already knows that the world they are coming into is filled with danger, that threats to their survival are sudden and frequent, and they are more likely to question the safety of human relationships and their own belonging in the world.

From the beginning of our existence, the electrical signals from another human impact our nervous system. We are inherently interconnected and deeply impacted by the traumatic experiences of the generations of women that came before us. We are designed to feel each other and to feed from each other, and when the messages we receive tell us that nourishment is not available or that the people we rely on to meet our needs are in fight, flight, or freeze, this shapes how we orient to safety, belonging within a family system, and being in relationship.

Generational trauma is real. We are born not only with a nervous system impacted by our mother's pregnancy, but also with imprint of our egg having traveled inside her body for the entirety of *her* human experience, impacted by stress hormones from the moment of her conception. And this is only one piece of how trauma is passed down from generation to generation.

Few of us are lucky enough to be carried in the wombs of women who have spent a lifetime in calm, healthy, regulation. Rather, the world we live in is intrinsically inhospitable and our fight for survival, and for freedom from oppression has been going on for hundreds of thousands of years. We've heard the stories of bodies being violated over and over again, and some of you reading have likely lived these stories yourselves.

Unfortunately, too many of us experience relational trauma that strips us of our agency and compromises our sense of ownership and safety in our skin. Not only do we face the ever-present threat of sexual and physical violence, just by having a body, but our image-obsessed culture is constantly reinforcing messages that our bodies are not good enough.

Fortunately, there is more research to support healing than ever before, and a number of mind-body therapies exist to help us break the cycle of generational, pre-verbal, and sexual trauma. The work of Bessel Van Der Kolk, author of *The Body Keeps the Score*[8], revolutionized the trauma healing industry, and we now know that our bodies store undischarged traumatic energy that can be accessed and released through targeted somatic interventions. Healing wounds of belonging, attachment trauma, and trauma from interpersonal violence requires more than talk therapy or retelling the experience until it magically makes sense in our mind. Thankfully, the medical and mental health industries are starting to catch on to the fact that you cannot treat the mind without working with the body.

Even without trauma therapy, we can individually lay the foundation for repairing our relationship to belonging in our bodies through body awareness practices and somatic exercises like yoga, qi gong, dance, music, drumming, and other rhythmic sensory input activities. Even swaying gently back and forth as you sit, or stand, is a rhythmic activity that can help you ground and support regulation.

For many of us, our bodies have been dishonored and disregarded for much of our lifetime. They have been a dumping ground for unresolved emotions and stress, and they've been neglected, under-appreciated, ignored, and even poisoned by sugar and chemicals that we ingest to soothe our cravings. Honoring your body doesn't necessarily mean you have to suddenly go on a juice fast or enroll in a detox program. Think of cultivating a loving relationship with your body more like making a new friend or going out on a date for the first time. One teacher of mine even invited us to relate to our bodies during an activity as if we were "courting the beloved." You can start slowly, just by bringing some caring attention to your body, as it already is in this moment, without wishing it were different. This may be a big shift in how you think about your body, so when you noticed that you have slipped into habitual patterns of dishonoring your body, gently notice this, and without judgment, consider how you can love your body now that you have woken up to this tendency. You *cannot* beat yourself into a better person. You *can* ask yourself, what would it be like to become friends with the body you already have, rather than shaming yourself or wishing it were different?

To set effective and fierce boundaries around your body, you have to fall in love with it again every day. You must believe your body is worth protecting and treating with dignity and utmost respect. And if you don't believe it yet, try pulling out a photograph of yourself as a baby or as a small child and make a commitment to believing it for that little one. You can tape this photograph on your bathroom mirror or keep it by your desk, and every time you see it say, silently or out loud, "you are worth protecting. You are worthy of care. You are enough."

Exercise 6.1: Hold Yourself with Dignity

Dignify your Posture: How you hold your body impacts your mindset. Body language is one of the strongest forms of nonverbal communication, and our posture is closely linked to our autonomic nervous system. Try it out for a minute. Adopt a posture that expresses an attitude of dignity and see if you can stay that way for a full minute. Notice areas of bracing or tensing in the body, and soften where you can, maintaining the dignified and upright posture. Show yourself that you are worthy of attention.

What do you notice in your body as you invite this quality of dignity and worthiness to be expressed through your posture?

Hero Pose: The Hero Pose is one of my favorite ways to "fake it 'til you make it." What qualities does your favorite hero possess? How would Wonder Woman hold herself in the face of harassment by text message? What posture did Rosa Parks take as she sat defiantly at the front of that bus. Next time your boundaries are under attack, or you simply feel exhausted and defenseless, pause, and take on a posture that  embodies the qualities of your favorite real life or fictional hero. Invite a sense of engagement in this physical stance, but also relax into it, as though the hero is doing the work for you. Again, invite a sense of engaged ease and alertness as you become the hero with your body. The mind will follow.

Reflection: What do you notice as you intentionally "put on" different postures in your body? How does the way you hold yourself impact your mood and energy?

You Deserve to Take Up Space

For much of my life, I have believed that I take up too much space. My body is too large, my energy is too big, my experience is too much. As a result, I've tried to confine myself so that I can "fit in," to the narrow space society has offered me. This has resulted in feelings of shame, self-criticism, chronic constriction of my muscles, habits of clenching and pulling inwards, and holding myself in a posture that closes me off to relationship and connection. There is a deep wounded part of me that believes it is not safe to occupy all of the space of my physical body, and that I have to tuck in my wings and be small and contracted to belong.

This belief likely comes from a combination of early traumas related to my adoption and experience of witnessing violence, and the toxic body shaming perpetuated by my peers and the media. Unraveling this subconscious programming has not been easy, and it is still an ongoing journey. The brief, informal mindful movement practices I learned in MBSR and taking the time each day to walk my dogs and intentionally release tension from my body have helped me tremendously. If I get lazy, however, and do not regularly attend to sensations in my body or disregard my need for movement and space to stretch my limbs and fully inhabit myself, I can easily fall into bad habits that trigger muscle aches and joint pain.

In my therapeutic and consulting work with clients and educators, I often offer brief guided movement activities to get things started or after we have dipped into a potentially triggering or highly emotional topic. Even though most people groan and express resistance to moving, because they say they are "too tired," once they do engage their body in gentle rhythmic motion, their attitude shifts. Not only is movement a primary intervention for regulating the nervous system after traumatic stimulation, but paying attention to the body moving also helps people shift attention away from their thoughts.

It is easy to forget that the body exists when we are working on a deadline, hyper-focused, or believing that others will judge us as unproductive if we take time to stretch or stand up from our desks. In truth, taking a moment to move the body increases blood flow to the brain and re-energizes the mind for increased focus and productivity. Furthermore, when we force ourselves to sit or are "stuck" in a position for long periods of time, this can activate our feelings of being trapped, especially if we have experienced confinement in previous trauma, and we can unknowingly retraumatize ourselves.

But the noticing of these habits gives us the opportunity to relate to them differently and to choose care for ourselves, even when it seems like a radical act. Any movement that opens up the body and allows you to take up space can be supportive. Additionally, rhythmic movements or those that alternate attention from left to right across the midline of the body, such as twists, side bends, or balancing poses done on both sides can be especially regulating.

Even if you do not have time to attend a formal yoga class or put out a yoga mat and get into pretzel shapes each day, it is possible to integrate body awareness and gentle intentional movements into your transitions and attitudes. Believe it or not, it is okay to stand and stretch during a meeting, go for a short walk at lunch, or step out into the hallway and fully extend your limbs. In fact, others will likely be envious of you for taking the time to honor your body, and they may even be inspired to follow your lead. Start by believing that you deserve to take up space, and that your body has a need for regular rhythmic movement that must be honored as a matter of survival.

Exercise 6.2: Take Up Residency in Your Body

Butterfly Breaths: Come into a standing posture with your feet hip-width apart and your knees bent slightly. Check the tilt of your pelvis, imagining that the pelvis is a bowl filled to the top with water, and you don't want the water to spill out the front or the back. Trace attention up the torso and back body, lengthening the spine. Relax the shoulders.

On an inbreath, lift the arms overhead. On the outbreath, lower the arms back to the sides. Repeat this exercise for at least five rounds of breath. You can play with the timing of your breath, synchronizing the movement with your arms. What happens as you slow down the movement and lengthen your breath? What happens as you speed up?

Warrior: Come into a wide lunge, with the arms extended parallel to the ground (you can also do this posture seated in a chair if needed). Turn the back foot so that it is perpendicular to the front foot. Sink down through your hips and extend through the fingertips of both hands.
You might even choose to turn the head and bring the eyes to the back hand, then turn the head again looking at the front hand, sending your attention through the length of your wingspan.

Soften the muscles of your shoulders, inviting a sense of engaged ease, not striving, or reaching for it, but resting into the posture with intention. Imagine you are both strong *and* receptive. Warrior postures allow you to practice softening the front of the body and strengthening the protective back of the body. Sustaining these poses for longer periods of time can help to balance the yin and yang, cultivate discernment, and to be open to giving and receiving while also remaining alert and skillful at protecting.

Five-Pointed Star/Vitruvian Man: For this practice, find a place where you can extend your body fully. Clear a space so that it is free of obstacles or pets who may get underfoot.

Start by coming into a standing posture with your legs a little wider than hip-distance apart. Bring your arms out to the sides so that your body makes a five-pointed star, like Leonardo DaVinci's Vitruvian Man. Allow yourself to take up all the space in your body, from fingertip to fingertip and from the top of your head down to the bottoms of your feet. This is where you live. You belong here. This is *your* body, and *you* get to decide what comes in and what stays out.

Now, shift your weight over to the left foot and lift the right foot off the ground, keeping the shape of the 5-pointed star. Balance here, as best you can for a few rounds of breath. Release this and shake out the arms for a moment. Then return to the 5-pointed star posture. Once you have restabilized on both feet, shift the weight over to the right foot and lift the left foot off the ground. Take a few rounds of breath here. Release and shake out the arms again.

Move with Abandon: Return to the 5-pointed star posture when you are ready. Begin moving your arms from side to side, front to back, and explore your "wingspan." How far does your body reach? Can you feel where your body begins and ends? You might even notice sensations occurring beyond the reach of your body.

Move into the space around you and take your body with you. Let yourself expand into the room, filling up all the available space with your body. Allow this movement to become a dance. Take care to stay present with your body and connected to sensation from moment to moment. Let your body move *you* however it wants to, abandoning all constraints and freeing yourself from the chains of shame. Dance like no one is watching. If it feels available, shake, pound, stomp, and expand your limbs fully and with raw, animal energy.

If you are willing, invite your voice to fill the space too. Are there words or sounds that want to come out of you? Are there things you need yourself to hear? You have the right to be as big as you need to be, to take all the space you need. What does it feel like to be a little less contained?

Reflection: As you interact with others and engage in your daily communications, bring attention to how you hold and move your body. Are you giving yourself permission to take up all the space you need or are you shrinking yourself to meet the needs of others?

The Body Scan

The Mindfulness-Based Stress Reduction program (MBSR) I have referenced is a course developed by Dr. Jon Kabat-Zinn at the University of Massachusetts Medical Center in 1979, designed to help participants use the wisdom of their body and mind to face stress, anxiety, depression, and chronic pain. It is a systematic training program in mindfulness meditation that meets for 2.5-hour sessions for 8 weeks, with a day-long silent retreat near the end of the program. Participants make a commitment to regular home practice and learn present-moment awareness, breathing techniques, movement meditations, yoga, mindful walking, and how to embody the principles of non-judgment, compassion, and non-reactivity in their daily lives.

The foundation of the course and daily home practice for the first four weeks is a 45-minute body scan meditation. The rationale behind regularly practicing the body scan is for participants to notice their relationship to attending to physical sensations and bring awareness to their habits of living in their heads and operating out of automatic pilot. The body scan also helps re-train the mind to attend to and sustain focus on what is happening in the body in the present moment, with an attitude of kindness. This repeated practice builds new neural pathways that allow access to body wisdom, which often reveals a deeper knowing and can help participants create more space between stimulus and response.

In my personal experience, the body scan is very useful in helping to reconnect with my felt experience in my body and to identify chronic patterns of tensing, bracing, and holding. Regularly listening to a guided body scan practice has helped me get to know and understand my body in a whole new way, and it is often one of the first practices I offer in group and individual sessions. Though everyone has a different experience with the body scan, many people find this practice to be quite relaxing and even use it to help them fall asleep at night.

Exercise 6.3: Body Scan

How to practice a body scan: While it is possible to do a body scan without guidance, I highly recommend using a recording to support you, as this allows you to rest your thinking mind. If you choose to listen to a body scan guided by someone else, I won't take it personally. However, please know that if you use the internet to do a blanket search for a "body scan," that there is a lot of junk and spiritual mumbo jumbo out there. Quality, secular body scans, based in present-moment awareness of sensations can be found on most MBSR teacher websites, but my recommendation is to access the downloadable "Gratitude Body Scan" recording at fierceboundaries.com.

When you are ready to do this exercise, set up your space so you can give yourself exquisite attention for the full 20 minutes. Turn off notifications on your devices, and let others know you are not to be disturbed.

You can practice seated or lying down on your back, or on your side, tucked into bed or just lying on a yoga mat or on the floor, or however you are most comfortable.

The goal of this exercise is not to achieve any special state, such as relaxation or falling asleep, but simply to be with your body and practice shifting attention out of thoughts and towards the physical sensations in your body with an attitude of nonjudgment, curiosity, and appreciation.

Starting at the top of the head or at the feet, scan attention through the body, one area at a time, noticing any sensations that arise. Pause and acknowledge each area by exploring sensations with curiosity and sending each body part some gratitude.

Fierceboundaries.com also includes a 35-minute MBSR body scan, a 5-minute standing body scan, and a 15-minute standing body scan with movement.

Reflection: What was it like to bring kind attention and gratitude to the different parts of your body in this way? What did you learn about your relationship to being with what is already happening in the body? How might you give yourself opportunities throughout your day to pause and appreciate your body?

A Note on Trauma and the Body Scan Practice

For some people who have survived trauma to the body, it may be very difficult or overwhelming to consider paying attention to sensations for a long period of time. Please know that this is completely normal, and that you can take this practice at your own pace and keep yourself in choice. There is nothing wrong with you if you do not feel a sense of relaxation or ease in this practice. If it is difficult to sustain awareness with physical sensations, I invite you to go slowly and to do whatever you need to do to keep yourself from becoming overwhelmed or triggered. For example, you may choose to practice sitting in a chair, rather than lying on the floor, or with your eyes open or closed. You might even choose a position that supports what your body needs, such as laying on your side, or resting on pillows.

As you listen to the guidance, if there are parts of the body that do not feel like they are safe places to rest your attention, it's just fine to shift attention to the breath or to another part of the body that feels neutral. It's important to remember that this is a *practice*, that there is no fixed outcome to achieve, and that it is an opportunity to befriend the body you already have, rather than trying to fix, change, or heal your body.

If you find yourself experiencing symptoms of traumatic arousal while practicing the body scan (such as rapid breathing, a feeling of panic, heart racing), pause the recording, open your eyes, and bring some movement back into the body. For those of us that may have experienced confinement, sometimes the instruction to become still in the body scan may make us feel like we are trapped or frozen. While there are benefits to allowing the body to rest in stillness, simmering in a freeze state or a feeling of paralysis can actually be re-traumatizing. Remember that there is no "doing it right" and you don't have to "follow the rules" to get the benefit of this practice. As best you can, allow yourself to have the experience you are having, and bring an attitude of kindness, care, and curiosity to what happens in your body when you attend to sensations in the present moment.

Finally, if you are an amputee or do not have sensation in part of your body, you can still practice the body scan as it is guided. When the instructions bring your awareness to a part of the body that has been lost, this can be an opportunity to notice your *relationship* to the missing or desensitized limb, and to make space for its memory. If there are no sensations, or emotions that arise, you can notice that. Whatever experience you have during the body scan, offer yourself some gratitude for bringing attention to your body and caring for yourself in this way. For those of us whose bodies have betrayed us, been violated, or contracted debilitating or terminal illness, the body scan is an opportunity to love and honor ourselves, just the way we are.

As someone who has practiced many body scans while experiencing severe physical pain, I understand that paying direct, sustained attention to areas of discomfort can be overwhelming. I invite you to take it slowly and to experiment with noticing sensations as pleasant and unpleasant, thoughts about wanting or not wanting sensations, and to recognize that you are already experiencing these sensations, even before you bring awareness to them. The body scan isn't about "releasing" tension or "relaxation" though these things may happen. In fact, it can be an opportunity to bring awareness to how our thoughts about pain and our resistance to pain can increase our suffering. Each time we shift our awareness from one part of the body to another, we are practicing "letting go," and this embodied practice can be great training for letting go of our thoughts as well.

Once you are familiar with the body scan practice, it can be done both formally and informally as an in-the-moment intervention to ground you in moments of stress or reactivity. The standing body scan practices can be especially useful for developing the practical skill of grounding in your body and managing stress if you are frequently in a standing posture in a high-pressure environment. I recommend practicing formally and consistently with the recording, daily for the first few weeks of your somatic awareness training. But if you can only practice from time to time, know that every small moment of honoring your body counts. If you need to, use this practice in small doses, as even baby steps can help you befriend your body and welcome yourself to belong inside your skin. Perhaps all you have time to do is pause while you are in the elevator or stuck in traffic and bring attention to the sensations of gravity in different parts of the body. Let this be enough. Befriending the body can be done even in the smallest moments, repeated many times.

Chapter 7: Take Agency

Cultivating somatic awareness through the body-based practices in the previous chapter can help you improve your physical literacy so that you are more easily able to listen to the wisdom of the body's knowing. Once you have an open channel of communication with your felt experience, it becomes possible to discern between what is helpful and what is harmful, and when you need to **take agency** and intervene on your own behalf.

Popular media, the billion-dollar self-help industry, Alcoholics Anonymous, and Hollywood movies have given us the mistaken impression that being "good enough" and emotional healing are fixed destinations that we can reach if only we follow the right path, take all the right steps, make sacrifices, stay disciplined, and keep our eye on the prize. We are led to believe that once we have arrived at this magical place where everything is better, we will find true love and live happily ever after for the rest of our lives. Rather than listen to the signals from our own bodies, we are encouraged to jump on the bandwagon, subscribe to popular prescriptive pathways, and listen to experts tell us what is wrong with us, what drug we should take, and how much money it will cost to fix it.

If we believe that healing comes from something *out there,* something outside of us, then it is a destination that can never be reached in a lifetime. But if we can reframe our language, change the story we are telling ourselves, and allow ourselves to honor our body's knowing and to tend to ourselves as needed from moment to moment, then real healing *from within* becomes possible. Rather than a destination to be reached, a protocol to be completed, or a status to be attained, perhaps healing means befriending and honoring your own unique experience, trusting your body to let you know what it needs, and speaking up for yourself when you need something different than what's socially expected.

Here's an example: After my back surgery, I could not sit for long periods of time because doing so would cause my abdominal muscles to clench and put pressure on my lumbar spine. However, I frequently found myself in classroom, meeting, or training situations where the unspoken expectation was to sit and listen to a lecture or presentation quietly, without moving, until it was over. Rather than taking a seat towards the front of the room or in the middle of an aisle as I might have once done, I started to choose a seat in the back, on the end of the row. Here, I could easily get up without disrupting the speaker, and stand behind my chair or at the back of the room for a time. I could even gently stretch or sway from side to side.

It may seem silly, but at first, I didn't realize I could do this, and I felt embarrassed to be the only one who couldn't sit still like everyone else. But my back pain and fear of reinjury made it a necessity. It was as if my life depended upon having the freedom to move and hold my body in a way that supported my health and safety. In fact, when I felt trapped in a sitting position for too long, I began to feel anxious, as the freeze state from being locked into a painful position in my body and the hyper-aroused state of wanting to jump up and flee conflicted with each other. This situation was a recipe for re-traumatization and a panic attack.

Eventually, I learned that it could be helpful to explain to the presenter ahead of time, or even to the whole group, that I was recovering from an injury and needed to take care of myself by sometimes standing and stretching and that doing so would allow me to be fully present. Speaking up for myself in this way wasn't easy at first, but I got used to it. I even found that taking agency in this way inspired other participants to take better care of themselves and gave them permission to move, which often led to *more* group cohesion and connection. I never once encountered a situation in which caring for myself was looked down upon or poorly received.

Widening the Window of Tolerance

The **window of tolerance** is a model coined by Dan Siegel in his 1999 book *The Developing Mind*. Siegel proposes that everyone has various intensities of emotional experience that we can comfortably experience, process, and integrate. This range is the "window" within which we experience a "zone of optimal arousal," or **regulation**. The wider our window, the higher our level of distress tolerance, and the easier it is to return to our zone of optimal arousal and regulation after an activating event.

Being "outside" of our window refers to the high-energy fight and flight states of **hyperarousal**, and the low-energy freeze, dissociate, and shut-down states of **hypoarousal**. When we are triggered or pushed beyond the threshold of our window of tolerance, we enter a state of **dysregulation**, or intensities of emotional experience that we cannot tolerate. Trauma narrows the window, and may cause us to become chronically dysregulated, either stuck in a state of hyper- or hypoarousal or swinging wildly between the two without returning to baseline. When a person has a narrow window of tolerance, even seemingly minor triggers can cause them to chronically dissociate, feel anxious, or suddenly become angry.

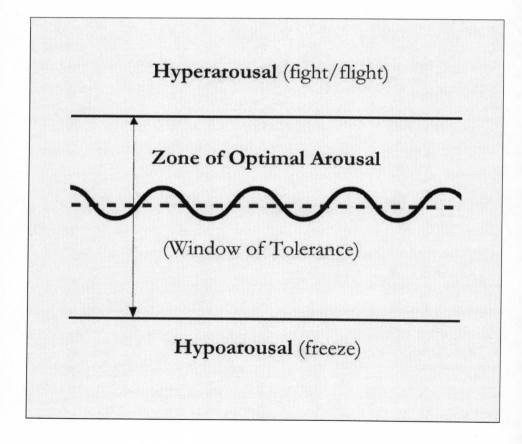

Window of Tolerance: The "optimal" zone of arousal for a person to function in everyday life. When a person is within their "window" they can effectively manage their emotions and regulate their nervous system.

Hyperarousal (fight/flight) – Anxious, angry, out of control, overwhelmed. The body wants to fight or flee to escape perceived danger.

Hypoarousal (freeze) – Spacey, zoned out, numbed, or frozen. The body wants to shut down or "play dead."

Common trauma-treatment protocol in psychotherapy includes both working with the memories and beliefs *and* widening the window of tolerance to support survivors in building the capacity to identify triggers, develop early intervention plans, and relate to their trauma with less reactivity. **Movement** and **taking agency** are two primary interventions for treating acute and chronic traumatic stress. The more often we practice moving in ways that honor what the body needs and making choices that support regulation, the more it is possible to reclaim ourselves and widen the window.

Agency (choice): Decision making is a function of the pre-frontal cortex (PFC), which shuts down when the amygdala fires and we perceive a threat. In crisis response and suicide intervention, counselors often encourage survivors to make small choices, such as, *would you like water or tea? Where would you like to sit, on the floor or on the couch? Would you like to use a blue or black pen?* Sometimes these choices are very difficult or overwhelming when someone has just experienced a severe threat, or they are operating out of a depressed or freeze state. But encouraging this choicefulness not only gives the survivor back a sense of agency, but it also brings the PFC back online and the nervous system can start to come back into a state of regulation.

Movement: For states of freeze or hypo-arousal, even small orienting movements (such as lifting a hand to receive a cup of tea or turning the head to look around the room and locate the exits) can support coming back into our window. When there is no agency regarding movement, survivors can easily become confined in their physical mobility, resulting in chronic pain.

States of hyperarousal, anxiety, and fight/flight can also be characterized by an intensity of physical sensations and traumatic energy in the body. Without moving the body and discharging this energy, this experience can overwhelm our systems and become too much. It may even feel like having the gas pedal and the brake pressed down at the same time, just like I did when I felt like I was "forced" to sit still in a meeting. With each re-activation of our fight/flight response, whether through thoughts, feelings, or external stimuli, the traumatic energy stored in the body increases, resulting in illness, chronic pain, feelings of panic and anxiety, and explosive reactivity. It is as if the body is an active volcano without steam vents or without an outlet for the building heat and churning lava. The pressure builds and builds until eventually the volcano erupts violently, causing massive destruction.

Practicing **choicefulness** with movement is a way to take agency and reclaim our right to inhabit our bodies with care and attention. When we deepen into a stretch or posture, taking as much time as we need, and with awareness and discernment, we are stepping into the driver's seat. We choose how much to fold forward and where to stop, and how long to hold our arms up over our heads and how quickly to lower them. I encourage you to access the 15-minute gentle movement practice available at fierceboundaries.com to practice choicefulness and taking agency with your body.

Working Skillfully with Discomfort

Second only to scarcity of time, physical discomfort is one of the largest stressors we face in our personal and professional lives. When I worked as an educator, life was regularly overwhelming, and my workload was unsustainable. Because I did not yet have effective boundary-setting or self-care practices in place, physical pain and sacrificing my mental health were constant. I was always bending over, maxing-out my attention, standing for hours on end, skipping meals, tending to the needs of everyone but myself, and even using the bathroom when I needed to was impossible. I had conditioned myself to push my body's needs to the bottom of the priority list. After all, the nature of my job was to "put the kids first."

When my pain flared up, my morale would plummet. I would spin into a spiral of negative thoughts about my inadequacy and brokenness, and I became short-tempered and easily overwhelmed. Little things, like a spill on the kitchen floor, or a grocery bag that was too heavy could push me to tears. I felt incapable of doing the things that gave me joy and a sense of purpose in the world, and the day-to-day functions of my many leadership roles were near impossible.

I've already told you the story of how this turned out for me in the end, but it doesn't stop me from still feeling frustrated that the system is set up this way in the first place. Discomfort and stress are inevitable, and we cannot control many of the conditions that create pain in our lives. However, what we can control is how we relate to the pain. This willingness to "accept the things I cannot change and the courage to change the things I can"[10] is a lifechanging philosophy relied on by many in recovery from alcohol addiction and forms the backbone of treatments for chronic pain and stress reduction.

During my first MBSR training, an instructors wrote the following equation on the board:

$$Pain + Resistance = Suffering$$
$$Pain \; {+ \; Resistance} \; = Pain$$

Without resistance, he claimed, pain is just pain. When we stop trying to make pain go away, and accept that it is already here, new possibilities for working with and tolerating discomfort can arise. Increasing our capacity to tolerate discomfort is very important if we are going to set effective boundaries. Getting familiar with the edges of our window of tolerance also gives us information about areas where we have been too permissive, or ways we have not taken control of a situation when perhaps we should have. Often, speaking up and taking agency is quite uncomfortable for people who have enabled or put others first for their whole lives.

For me, not responding to a text message or email from my ex takes a whole new level of being with the difficult feelings and urgent sensations that accompany resisting the urge to engage. In research on positive habit change, building the capacity to tolerate discomfort and **surf the urge**[11] is a critical component to success. The more we are able to be with the difficult sensations of cravings and impulses and allow them to arise and pass without giving in, the fiercer we can defend ourselves against temptation, addiction, patterns of unhealthy coping, and cycles of abuse.

In the following exercise, we'll turn gently towards difficult sensations in our bodies, notice resistance, and experiment with different techniques for working with difficulty. As you do this practice, make sure you stay in choice and return again and again to that foundational question: *How can I best take care of myself, given what is arising?*

The first time you do this exercise, I encourage you to use the 9-minute audio recording available at fierceboundaries.com.

Exercise 7.1: Awareness of Difficult Sensations

Sit in an upright and dignified posture that supports paying attention, either on a cushion or on a chair. Bring attention to the body in space, and attend to posture, making sure the body is self-supporting, and not leaning into the future or slumped into the past. Welcome yourself and give attention a few moments to settle.

Stabilize attention by taking a few full breaths all the way in and out, and then come to rest on an anchor of your choosing, either the sensations of breath, sounds coming and going, or gravity in the body.

When you are ready, shift your attention towards some area of the body where there is tension or some intensity of sensation. Bring a spirit of kindness and inquiry to this area, notice any judgment or resistance that arises, and see if you can allow yourself to have the experience you are having, just for a few moments.

There are three ways offered to work with discomfort in the body.

1. Bring the full focus of your attention to the area of difficulty. Investigate with kindness and curiosity and see if you can explore the sensations without bracing and tensing against them. Welcome them, as best you can. After all, the discomfort is already here, and you are already tolerating it. Invite the breath to fill this area of discomfort, filling the cells with new oxygen on the inbreath, and softening and releasing on the outbreath. Notice density, texture, size, shape. Name the sensations you feel with a mental note, such as throbbing, piercing, stabbing, quivering, pulling, pressure, tingling, tightness.

2. If the sensations become overwhelming, shift your attention back to another anchor in the present moment, such as the breath, sound, or neutral sensations in another part of the body. Let yourself stabilize attention here, and then when you are ready, return attention to the original area of discomfort and investigate again.

3. In some cases, it may be necessary to move the body to alleviate discomfort. If you choose to do this, first set the intention to move, then move with mindfulness and care. Notice how sensations shift and see if you can keep your attention with the area of discomfort and notice the changing nature of sensations here. Once the discomfort or pain has been alleviated, you may wish to return to the original posture and again bring a spirit of investigation and curiosity to this part of the body.

Complete this practice by releasing your attention from the area of discomfort and returning to rest on your anchor. Give yourself an opportunity to take a few full rounds of breath. You may even wish to congratulate yourself, and to thank yourself for tending to the body in this way.

Reflection: What did you notice as you brought attention to areas of discomfort? What was challenging? How did you meet these challenges as they arose? What do you notice now as you reflect upon this practice? How might you build these ways of working with difficulty into your workday?

The Power of Choice

In 2019, I had the opportunity to attend a week-long workshop at the Omega Institute with Jon Kabat-Zinn and his son, Will Kabat-Zinn, called *The Way of Awareness*. For much of the time that we were together, we alternated between 30 minutes of sitting meditation and 30 minutes of mindful walking.

For walking meditation, Dr. Kabat-Zinn instructed us to choose a 10–12-foot straight pathway and walk back and forth along that pathway, slowing down the act of walking enough that we could note the *lifting, moving, placing* of each foot. When we reached the end of our runway, we were invited to pause and gather our attention, then note *turning, turning, turning* and continue walking back in the other direction. He reminded us that there was no destination, and each footfall was a kind of "controlled falling." We were to "take up residency in the feet," and to release attachment to an outcome.

So, every half hour, all 200 of us emptied out of the meditation hall in a hoard, and poured silently onto the lawn, where we paced back and forth slowly in every direction. Other visitors to the Omega campus, who were not part of our group, walked through the haphazard ambling crowd, babbling, and scrolling on their phones, mindlessly dodging the random walking meditators, leading us to joke later about who the real "zombies" were.

I did not like walking meditation, and every time we were supposed to do it, I noticed in myself an impulse to slip away and escape while no one was watching. Similar to the desire to flee that gripped me when I first began sitting on a meditation cushion in silence, the formality of the practice, and the expectation of slow, restricted movement felt like a prison for my body. It also seemed to exacerbate the numbness and tension in my left leg, where my sciatic nerve was still recovering from my microdiscectomy. The feeling of physical confinement and nerve paralysis, combined with my wish to impress Dr. Kabat-Zinn, a teacher I greatly admired, led to an overwhelming increase in anxiety, almost to a state of panic.

One evening, I had the opportunity to bring this experience into the Q&A session with Dr. Kabat-Zinn, who replied with a scoff, "you need to let go of attachment to an outcome."

I felt my cheeks flush with anger and the rise of bile in my throat. "What if what's needed is for my body to move more quickly because there is some kind of traumatic rage energy moving through me?" I said, snapping back at him and trying not to cry. "Is it possible to be mindful of walking at a faster pace?"

He smiled gently, seeing the emotion in my face, and softened his tone. "At first it really should be practiced slowly, if possible, so that you can get to know the discomfort and study your resistance. But who knows?" he said, shrugging. "Why don't you try it and see?" *(Author's Note: I did not realize it at the time, MBSR is not a trauma-sensitive program and Dr. Kabat-Zinn is not a particularly trauma-informed teacher, though I believe that in recent years he has gotten more educated on appropriate strategies for working with survivors. As much as I respected his wisdom, teachers I would work with later would help me understand the need to honor my body's traumatic history and that certain meditation traditions and practices were not suitable for me without trauma-sensitive modifications).*

For the rest of the week, I gave myself permission to diverge from the instructions that were followed by the other 199 participants. I took the opportunity to walk away from the mob and down towards the lake, where I could be out of sight and have space away from the expectations of formal practice. I immediately noticed a sense of peacefulness and safety that washed over me once I was on my own. Alone, I was free to move in my own direction, and to follow my own inner knowing. I continued the practice of walking meditation as instructed, bringing awareness to the sensations of my feet hitting the ground, noticing when my attention was pulled into thinking or striving, and then returning to the movement of my body. Now that I was alone, it was much easier to be with my own experience, rather than being focused on the experiences of others and my worries about how I was being perceived.

Over the course of that week, I played around with the practice. Sometimes, I moved quickly, sometimes slowly. Sometimes I stayed with the crowd, and other times I wandered towards the lake where I could just be with myself. I started to notice that when I was surrounded by others, and by the confines of expectations and a group practice environment, I contained and restricted myself, and this led to anxiety and more cramping and bracing in my legs.

In a group setting, I was determined to get it right, and to impress — an instant trigger. But when I was alone, it was safe to be my truest self and I could move freely and let go of worries about what others thought of me. Walking became a dance. This was indeed rich territory for investigating my habits and core beliefs around doing it like everyone else, being told how to move and hold my body, and releasing attachment to a destination and an outcome. At the heart of my learning was this essential question: *is it safe to honor my body's needs around others?*

When I reflect on this question now from the writer's seat, I recognize that ignoring my body's needs and signals in workplace and relational contexts has been the source of much of my chronic pain, illness, and injury. To meet the expectations of administrators, bosses, and romantic partners how many of us have stayed sitting, even when our bodies were crying to stand? How often have we remained hunched over our desks, plowing through shoulder tightness and neck strain to meet a deadline? How many of us have sat frozen or paralyzed as someone threatens or verbally abuses us, locking that terror into our tissues, and condemning ourselves to a lifetime of guilt and shame. Why didn't I try to stop him? Why didn't I say "no?" How often have rumination and toxic relationships taken up residency in our minds, while we stiffen and tense our bodies against the threat of a person who is not even there in the room with us? How many of us are re-traumatizing ourselves daily, by forcing stillness, marinating in the fear of the memories that live in our muscles and bones, locking ourselves inside our minds, just to keep ourselves safe?

That week at Omega, I learned that when practiced with choicefulness, walking meditation can offer freedom from the prison of our habitual thought patterns and limiting beliefs. Giving ourselves permission to take up residency in our bodies, to take agency over our own experience, and to move with intention, helps us re-prioritize our own wellbeing and reclaim our birthright to move through the world in our own way. With every intentional step, we come home to ourselves.

Exercise 7.2: Walking Meditation

Choose a straight pathway that is about 10-12 feet in length. You can do this practice with shoes on, or barefoot, indoors, or outdoors, on a smooth surface or a rough one. Set a timer for 10, 20, or 30 minutes, and walk slowly, back and forth along this pathway, inviting yourself to let go of reaching a destination or accomplishing a specific outcome.

As you lift, place, and move each foot, note *lifting, placing, moving*. When you notice that attention has shifted into thinking, striving, or planning, you can pause and gather your attention, bring awareness back to the sensations in your feet and legs, and noting the movement of the legs. When you reach the end of your 10–12-foot runway, you can pause and gather attention again, and note *turning* as you reorient the body to go back in the other direction.

If you notice resistance, discomfort, aversion, or unpleasant sensations or emotions, see if you can allow this to inform your inquiry into your experience, rather than trying to change the experience to make it more pleasant. For the duration of this practice, take up residency in your feet, arriving at your destination each time you place your foot on the ground.

Reflection: What was it like to practice mindful walking? What did you learn about how you relate to moving through the world and arriving at your destination?

This is your body, and choosing how your body moves is your birthright, and something that no one should ever take from you. If your body has been violated in the past, and your movement restricted by force, I am so sorry that you experienced this, and it was absolutely wrong for you to be treated this way. Walking meditation may be a practice that gives you an opportunity to reclaim yourself, but please take care of yourself as it's possible that stored traumatic memories and undischarged energy may re-surface. If this happens, seek guidance from a mental health professional, and get support. It doesn't mean this practice isn't potentially helpful, but it does mean that you should not navigate what arises on your own.

The renowned teacher Thich Nhat Hanh has written entire books on the subject of walking meditation. During his lifetime, he amassed many followers who would amble behind him through the gardens and pathways of Plum Village, deepening their practice of "arriving at their destination with every step[12]." If this practice resonates for you, I highly recommend you explore some of Thich Nhat Hanh's exquisite and practical teachings.

I have a different relationship to walking meditation now than I did when I first practiced at Omega. Having once been confined to a wheelchair, this practice gives me an opportunity to savor the pleasure and privilege of being able to walk. Having the ability to self-propel in a world that is full of limitations and barriers is such a gift. Although it is not generally a part of my daily formal practice, walking meditation is now one of my favorite informal ways to take agency over my own experience, force myself to slow down, and refocus my attention on my relationship to being alive.

These days, every time I find myself waiting in line, pumping gas, or if I am standing still for long periods of time, I use this extra time as an opportunity to take a few mindful steps and tend to myself, rather than scrolling Facebook or checking my email. Without anyone else being impacted and without disrupting the flow of things, I can shift my weight from one foot to the other, focus on the sensations in the soles of my feet, check in with balance, feel the earth beneath me, and reclaim my attention.

When you tune in and honor the needs of your body and choose movement even when it is contrary to the unspoken expectations of your environment, you are committing a radical act of social justice advocacy. Especially in leadership or parenting roles, having the courage to stand or stretch your body can be transformational, not just for yourself, but also for the people around you. When you are willing to publicly tend to your own experience, show care and compassion to your body, and even make time and space for others to do the same, you are sending the message to the world that your health, balance, and wellbeing matter.

Part 2:

Reclaim Your Heart

Chapter 8: The Wisdom of the Wounded Heart

When I experienced my first real break up after a long-term relationship in college, I finally realized what people meant when they talked about "heartbreak." I had experienced being "hurt" before, and already knew well the emotional pain of rejection and the emptiness of longing to be a part of something that felt safe and enduring. But getting "dumped" by my boyfriend, Mark, toward the end of my sophomore year was a different kind of rupture – the kind where the bottom falls out from underneath of you and your insides plummet into the pit of despair and shatter when they hit the bottom into a million shards of broken dreams.

I wallowed for weeks, skipping class, and staying in bed, unable to mobilize for anything other than a trip to the bathroom. Everything I had hoped for and envisioned for the future had evaporated. Without Mark in my life, I saw no reason to go on. Without him, I was nothing.

Much of that time is a blur, and I don't remember many details from that semester, but what I do remember is the physical pain of my broken heart – the crushing weight of loneliness in my chest, the ripped-open feeling of a soul-splitting wound, the bursting of my grief through layers of muscle and bone, the fire-red and swollen skin around my tear-filled eyes, the festering of anger churning in my empty gut, and the throbbing of my temples as I begged the Universe to *please* bring him back to me.

Looking back, I see that I was drowning because I didn't yet have the wisdom or skills to guard my tender heart with healthy boundaries. After a lifetime of not fitting in, and out of desperation for a fairy tale romance, I had left myself unguarded, with the gates to my heart wide open. When my knight in shining armor came along, I was so astonished that he wanted my heart that I didn't hesitate to give it away. I made myself permeable and exposed. Once he was inside my fortress, I locked the gates behind him and trapped him within my undying, non-negotiable, un-boundaried love.

It's no wonder that he suffocated in there. And it's no wonder that to take himself back he had to break down the walls of my heart and split me open to extract himself.

For weeks, I languished in the sea of grief, with barely enough spiritual strength to even try to keep my head above water. Then one day, hunger finally got the better of me and I took a shower and emerged from my den of darkness to brave the dining hall. It was springtime, and when I stepped outside, the fresh air hit my lungs, the sunshine warmed my skin, and the birds warbled as if the whole world had suddenly come alive again.

One day at a time, I found small reasons to live *my own* life. With the help of the college guidance counselor, I made plans with my professors to get caught up on my work and refocused the energy from my heartbreak into maintaining my grade point average. Each paragraph I wrote, each centering breath I took, and each moment of laughter with a friend over French fries and soft serve ice cream was a baby step out of the depths of depression. I was surprised to find that even though I lost myself for a while, and my heart would always be scarred from where it was torn apart, I was still essentially *me* without Mark – a wiser, stronger, whole human with a new story to tell of love, loss, and finding my way back home.

Honestly though, it took me years to stop wanting him back or even consider the possibility of allowing someone else to get close. There was a Mark-shaped hole in my life that no one else would ever be able to fill, and an impenetrable fortress of stone around my heart with no entrances or exits. If I never let anyone get that close, then maybe I could protect my tender heart from being shattered again.

So, I swung completely to the other side of the pendulum and became hyper-independent and wild, living an adventuring life and traveling alone, convincing myself that I didn't need a man to be happy. I spent the decade of my twenties mostly friendless, aimless, and disconnected from my family, free as a bird and unburdened by the relational drama that seemed to plague everyone else. In some ways I was happy enough, but there was a gnawing ache in my heart and a deep loneliness I could never shake.

Eventually, my desire to become a mother pulled me back into the dating world, and out of desperation for connection, I once again bared my heart to a man. I was an all-or-nothing kind of girl, with my heart either rigidly defended or gaping open, soft, and exposed. I did not know a middle ground. And I did not have the self-confidence to believe that someone would want me if I was at all guarded. I also did not know at the time that my codependency, relational anxiety, and black and white thinking were trauma responses, and that making my heart available to an abusive, addicted, depressed man was etched in my DNA.

Years after my devastating college breakup, with my heart aching and raw from the grief of divorce, I offered to be the "demo" client for an equine assisted psychotherapy training that was part of my graduate counseling course in eco-therapy. The horse chosen for me was a dappled gray mare named Misty, and as soon as I entered the round pen, she ambled up next to me and stood in front of me lining her chest up with my heart. Instinctively, I placed the palms of my hands on Misty's side, where I could feel her ribs moving back and forth with the rhythm of her big, slow breaths. Her body was warm and welcoming and soft, and beneath my palms I could even feel the deep pulsing of her heart. Tears started to trickle down my cheeks, and I wrapped my arms around her, resting my face against her back.

The warmth of her body softened everything that was compressed into a tight ball inside me. My daughter's father was growing more depressed and bitter towards me day by day. During our marriage, whenever I experienced an emotion of my own, he managed to turn it around, make it about him, and get defensive, leading to a massive blowout argument that lasted for hours until we were both exhausted and emotionally drained. There had been no space for my heart or feelings to be acknowledged, and containing myself for years had led me to a state of constant anxiety and resentment that was still with me as we tried to navigate the landmine-strewn territory of coparenting. These conditions were what brought me into the round pen that day and led me to eagerly volunteer for the session.

Our facilitator guided me in a standing body scan where I progressively relaxed my muscles starting at the top of my head and sweeping my attention down to the bottom of my feet. As I focused my attention on different parts of my body, Misty leaned into me and allowed me to rest more and more of my weight onto her. By the time the body scan was complete, I was audibly crying and had draped my entire upper body across her back and let myself become heavy, and Misty did not pull away. I was surprised by the release of emotion and confused. I was relieved to be free from my marriage, so how had my anger and anxiety turned into grief?

"Thank you," I whispered to her as she supported me with her massive, solid, unwavering presence. "Thank you for staying."

The wave of emotion welled up and hit me suddenly, spilling out like water from a broken dam. I sobbed and heaved with big waves of sadness. Still, Misty didn't flinch or give any indication that my emotions were too big or my energy too much for her. I looked up and saw the other graduate students gathered around us, looking on in awe, many of them also in tears.

Then, I was openly weeping in a way that I'd never allowed myself to do in front of anyone before. As I poured my heart onto this gentle, comforting creature, I realized that I wasn't grieving the loss of my ex, or even the loss of the life I had dreamed of when we married. I was grieving the loss of the birth mother I had never known. I was grieving because I had been left by the one person who was supposed to hold me and carry me and never let me go. And because she left me, I'd spent my life longing to be held and witnessed by someone who would stay, even when I cried. And no one had.

Grief, it turns out, is not specific to a singular relationship. When the doorways to grief are unlocked, they can open you up to all the unintegrated sadness in your past. Because I was so little when I was adopted, I never grieved the loss of my birth mother when it happened, as I had no way to process the enormity of my abandonment and was celebrated for my resilience, so it made sense to bury my sadness. But that loss was still in there, like a child curled up in the fetal position in a forgotten corner, weeping unseen and unnoticed for most of her lifetime.

I wrapped myself around the horse's neck, and nuzzled my face into her mane, imaging that I was curling up around that wounded, hidden little one. I started to hum and sway back and forth, the gentle movement of my body following the rhythmic motion of Misty's breathing.

A final hum melted into a sigh and then a swelling of joy in my heart bubbled into laughter. Misty bent her neck around to nibble at an itch on her side, and I instinctively reached out and gave her a scratch with my long fingernails. She whinnied and stretched her head and neck towards the sky in pleasure, and the onlooking students laughed and emitted a spontaneous, collective, "awww."

Then, Misty snorted and shook her mane, sending ripples across her skin, and stepped gently away. The facilitator opened the gate and held out a box of tissues and led us over to our circle of chairs to debrief the session.

The Impact of Early Experience

Despite the heartache we cause each other, human beings are drawn together like magnets and designed for togetherness. We are born to be completely dependent on our caregivers, and we are unable to survive without the protection, nourishment, and love of another human. Our systems are designed to feed each other, feel each other, and to intuit each other's needs. This inter-dependence and co-regulation are so deeply engrained in our biology that a baby's cry evokes cognitive conflict in our brains, forcing us to shift attention and focus on meeting the baby's needs. We are deeply connected to each other, and entirely unable to survive alone.

In the first years of our lives, we create maps of how we believe the world works, with data gathered from our senses and our core experiences, that become stored in our subconscious mind, cellular memory, and muscle tissues. These **core beliefs** are formed by our interactions with primary caregivers, by observing their patterns and behaviors, and by our resulting sense of belonging and worthiness within our family system. In response to the conditions that exist around us, we develop strategies for getting our needs met and establish boundaries around our hearts to protect ourselves from emotional wounding.

Secure attachment occurs when we experience reliable attention and support, and our needs are met. **Insecure attachment** occurs when there is a disruption in the process of bonding between the child and their primary caregiver. This is a type of trauma, and may take the form of abuse or neglect, or it may be more subtle, such as lack of affection or response from a caregiver. **Trans-generational trauma** occurs when wounds are passed down through our genes and behaviors, from generation to generation, because there has not been resolution or healing. Epigenetic research[13] on trans-generational transmission of traumatized behaviors in mammals even shows that exposure to stress hormones in-utero permanently impacts the behavior of offspring, even when those offspring are never exposed to the traumatized parent.

In an environment of neglect, abuse, mental illness, financial strain, or unpredictability, we may decide no one can be trusted, everyone leaves us if we need too much, all men are violent, or it's not safe to be close because inevitably the people you are close to will hurt you. Or maybe we learn that we must work hard to earn love, that survival means staying on guard permanently, or that to keep our family safe we cannot ask for help, and that resting or relying on others means putting ourselves in danger. If we learned long ago that our needs were too much for our caretakers, we may unintentionally ignore pain in our own bodies, or put ourselves in positions that create physical discomfort, and dismiss our own need for physical safety and ease in favor of taking care others. Our patterns of holding or tensing in our bodies can become habitual, or chronic, and we can get "locked in" to certain behaviors, movements, or strategies that perpetuate this belief of "my needs don't matter."

In the 1960s and 70s, researchers Mary Ainsworth and John Bowlby[14] theorized that based on our early experiences with our caregivers, we develop "schemas" or beliefs about ourselves as worthy or unworthy of care and attention, and others as reliable or unreliable sources of support. They recognized four **attachment styles** which inform our behavior and our approach to relationships throughout our lives. Data suggests that approximately 50% of adults are **securely** attached, 20% are **anxious (ambivalent)**, 25% are **avoidant (dismissive)**, and the remaining 5% are **fearful (disorganized)** in their attachment style. These are not meant to be defined as fixed states, and you may not fall cleanly into one style or another, but all of us exist somewhere on the continuum.

Secure: Your primary caregiver was likely a stable and predictable source of love and acceptance. They responded to your changing needs and were able to communicate safety non-verbally and manage and express their emotions. In adult life, people with a secure attachment style:
- Are comfortable with intimacy.
- Are resilient, can bounce back quickly from adversity.
- Are often able to set appropriate, healthy boundaries.
- Feel safe, stable, and satisfied in close relationships.
- Can balance dependence and independence.

Anxious (Ambivalent): Your primary caregiver was likely inconsistent. At times they may have been unavailable and distracted, or they may have been engaged and responsive. You may have been uncertain whether your needs would be met. In adult life, people with an anxious attachment style:
- Crave closeness but struggle to trust or rely on their partner.
- Can be overly dependent, may feel threatened by too much space.
- Have a chronic fear of rejection.

- Have difficulty maintaining healthy boundaries out of desperation to belong and a need for validation of their worthiness.
- May need constant reassurance from their partner, may achieve this through manipulation, being needy.
- Define their self-worth by how they are being treated in relationship. Always evaluating and tracking for this information.

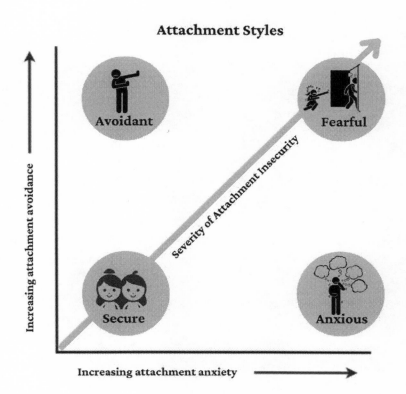

Attachment Styles

Avoidant (Dismissive): Your parent was likely unavailable or rejected you during your infancy. You learned to self-soothe because your needs were not adequately met. A deep fear of abandonment leads you to avoid relationships and reject intimacy later in life, as a way of protecting yourself from getting hurt. In adult life, people with an avoidant attachment style:

- May end relationships to regain a sense of freedom.
- Are highly self-sufficient and may withdraw when someone tries to get close.
- Feel they do not need relationships and that they do better on their own.
- May set overly rigid boundaries or build walls that isolate and keep people away to protect themselves from being hurt, which they feel is inevitable if they let someone get too close.
- May feel triggered or violated when someone crosses a boundary.
- Seek out independent partners who keep their distance emotionally.

Fearful (Disorganized): Your primary caregiver may have been an unpredictable source of fear *and* comfort and may have been dealing with their own unresolved trauma. Or, your parent may have ignored or overlooked your needs, creating confusion and disorientation in how you feel about relationships. In adult life, people with a disorganized attachment style:

- May be controlling or untrusting of their partner.
- May abuse alcohol or drugs and be prone to violence.
- Desire intimacy and find it confusing and scary.
- Swing between feelings of love and hate.
- Could feel unworthy of love and be terrified of getting hurt.
- Boundaries are extremely confusing and swing back and forth between being overly rigid or non-existent.

Healthy and unhealthy relationships can impact attachment styles over time, and because of the brain's inherent neuroplasticity, it is possible to change how you relate to belonging in the world by cultivating somatic awareness, especially in reference to the heart-mind connection. Our *thoughts* about belonging in relationship are informed by our past attachment experiences and worries about the future. Our *emotions* are informed by our thoughts, but we experience emotions only in the present moment. Healing attachment wounds involves integrating the heart and mind by matching up the memory of the core experience that created the relational wound with a nervous system that is balanced, calm, and understands that the danger has passed.

Getting to know your attachment style and tending to your wounded parts with somatic awareness can open the possibility of deeper connection that is safe *and* protected – in which *you* are the gatekeeper of your heart's energy.

Reflection: What is your attachment style? What does your attachment style reveal about your capacity to set and enforce healthy boundaries? What was the missing experience for you as a child, when you were deciding how relationships worked?

<hr>

Exercise 8.1: Soothing Somatic Holds

Place a hand on your heart and feel the sensations of holding yourself and being held. Notice the weight of your hand, and any messages that your heart has for your hand or your hand for your heart.

Wrap your arms around each other, holding onto your upper arms with each hand and just resting there in that gentle embrace. You might even say to yourself as you're giving yourself this physical touch, I've got you. I'm right here. I'm not going anywhere.

Rest your face in your hands. Place your elbows on the table and make a cradle with your hands, where you can plop your face down and give yourself the softness and the receiving that are available from your open hands.

Squeeze the back of your neck and your shoulders, and massage down your arms, torso, thighs, and calves. Starting again at the top of your body, sweep your hands in soft brushing strokes across your skin, sweeping away any old or stagnant energy from the body.

Listen with Your Heart

The human heart is not only a tender, electrical, blood-pumping organ, but it has a network of 40,000 neurons that function autonomously, like a small brain[15]. The heart's energetic field, measured by an electrocardiogram, is more than 5000 times greater in strength than the field generated by the brain and can be detected anywhere on the surface of the skin. In humans, this electromagnetic field can be detected three feet away from a body, and even farther when we are experiencing strong emotions. For horses, this field is five times more powerful than ours, and can extend almost thirty feet away.

This makes horses great therapists because of their enormous hearts' capacity to come into coherence with human nervous systems. Horses' hearts, just like humans', have a measurable electromagnetic field that communicates a tremendous amount of information to the brain. This information exchange happens both inwardly (to the brain) and outwardly (to the electromagnetic fields of other mammals), and acts as a sort of sensory antenna, continuously giving and receiving information (such as mood-states, physical condition, level of arousal, and intentions).

Without having to purposefully communicate, verbalize, or know background information, all mammals continuously give and receive these energetic signals to those around us, while at the same time we respond to the electromagnetic information we receive from the nervous systems and heart rates of others in proximity to us. We belong together, we feel each other, and we are essentially inseparable, whether we like it or not.

When we experience distressing or negative emotions, such as grief, betrayal, or exile, our heart rate variability becomes disordered and "**incoherent.**" This means that our cognitive functions (such as attention, memory, problem solving, and perception) are impaired. This can result in the release of excess cortisol to our blood stream, as well as higher levels of stress, anxiety, apathy, and depression.

On the other hand, when we feel positive emotions, our heart rate variability becomes "coherent" and balances the body's systems, allowing for creativity, problem solving, and an increase in our ability to learn, think clearly, remember, and make wise choices. "**Cardiac coherence**" means our nervous, cardiovascular, hormonal, and immune systems are in balance, which enhances our resilience and our overall physical and mental health.

The neurons in our heart as well as others in our gut send information to the brain via the **Vagus Nerve**. This nerve wanders all over the body, overseeing a vast range of functions and communicating sensory and motor impulses to every organ. Its main functions are to bring us back into a state of calm and maintain coherence. Toning exercises for the Vagus Nerve improve **heart rate variability** (a measure of the beat-to-beat changes in heartrate) and make it easier to bounce back from stressful situations. This can be done with deep breathing, humming, singing, laughing, yoga, and acupuncture.

The extension of our electromagnetic field beyond the boundary of our skin is one of the reasons that our nervous systems are deeply contagious and highly susceptible to being negatively affected by the energies and emotions of others, especially those with whom we are in an intimate relationship. In codependent relationships, our heart energies can become enmeshed or entangled with each other, and we may have trouble discerning what emotions and reactions belong to us, and what belongs to the other person. When two electromagnetic fields are incoherent (for example, there is an intense electromagnetic field next to a milder one), the milder one is attracted to the more intense one and gets in tune with it. When coherent fields are pulled together, they generate a larger and more powerful coherent field. This is why we can so easily "lose ourselves" inside of abusive relationships.

This heart-mind resonance allows us to set new boundaries that offer the opportunity to be the gatekeeper, and to practice skillful discernment based on real-time information (rather than past experience) around who and what we allow into our heart space. When you practice directing your attention and then distinguishing your energy from others, you can use this information to set boundaries that help you regulate yourself amid turmoil, cultivate positive emotions in a toxic environment, and be an influence of calm, responsive, stability for others.

Exercise 8.2: Heart-focused Breath

Bring attention to the area of your heart. Place both hands on your heart or one hand on your heart and one hand on your belly. Allow the attention to settle with the physical sensations of your hands making contact with your body. Notice the rhythm of the movement of the breath.

Become aware of the energetic state of the heart. You might notice a quality of quivering, softness, clenching, heaviness, lightness, openness, hardening. Whatever arises, see if you can welcome it, just as you would welcome an invited guest. Allow the hands to soothe the heart and notice that you are both holding yourself and being held. Notice any emotions that arise and see if you can breathe into the space around your heart, making a little more room for all your experience.

Now, bring awareness to the expansion and contraction of your breath around your heart. Breathe in for a count of five and breathe out for a count of five. Take at least three full rounds of breath in this intentional way.

Reflection: What was it like to bring attention to the qualities of the energy around your heart? What did you notice? How can you best care for yourself, given what showed up in that exercise?

I invite you to notice over the coming days and weeks what happens as you enter and leave other people's heart space. Slow down and bring attention to your cardiac coherence and the qualities of energy around your heart in various interactions and at various distances from others. If you are engaged in a difficult conversation or conflict with someone, take a step back and give yourself some physical space. Take a few grounding breaths and center yourself before continuing.

The heart knows so much more than we give it credit for. Honor the wisdom of your wounded places. Listen inwardly, connect with the rhythm of your heartbeat, and hold yourself with the care and regard you did not get to receive when you were young. Let yourself know over and over again that you are worth protecting. You are worthy of safety. You are worthy of relationships that are nourishing, and it is okay to set boundaries to keep your heart from getting ripped apart.

When I married my ex, I didn't listen to my heart. I married him driven by my anxious-avoidant attachment style and because my beliefs about my worthiness told me that no one else would want me. And then I settled into a life of pushing my needs to the back burner, carrying all of his emotional burden, and fighting desperately to make him stay, even though he sucked the joy out of every room. If only I could have heard my heart screaming, perhaps I could have protected myself a little more.

What kind of healing might be possible if more of us learned to navigate the world by feeling the wounded places in our hearts and listening to their wisdom? Could we find our way home to ourselves and each other with a little less rumination and heartbreak? After all, look at what animals can do with the electromagnetic information from their hearts. Migratory birds use magnetic clues to guide their journey during migration. Sea turtle hatchlings a few minutes old can sense the direction of the earth's magnetic field. Cattle and some species of deer tend to situate themselves along a north-south axis, except when they are too close to high-voltage power lines, which they'll orient to instead. When we learn how to listen, human hearts also possess this depth of interconnectedness and knowing how to stand together and orient ourselves to the world.

The combination of knowing your attachment style and accessing the wisdom of the heart gives you agency and space for discernment, as well as the capacity to know when you are acting from a place of childhood wounding rather than present moment experience. The sensations and rhythm of your heart offer real-time information from your environment, and listening to what your nervous system is telling you gives you the opportunity to recognize and step out of core patterning and opens the possibility of connecting you more deeply to yourself and others.

Perhaps connecting more deeply to the electromagnetic signals coursing through our bodies and getting to know the sensitivity of our heart's field can help us navigate the world and set boundaries that are informed by a deeper knowing. We can use our heart-mind literacy and our understanding of heart coherence to place wise boundaries around our own experience and reclaim ourselves from generations of attachment trauma, even when we are surrounded by dysregulation.

The purpose behind sharing the theoretical basis of attachment and my own attachment exploration is to shed light on an accessible process for reparenting the wounded little one inside of those of us who have experienced the impact of generational trauma. Looking at your own tendencies, and examining your attachment style can give you information so that you can then ask yourself, as I did so many times in the course of this journey, *how can I best support myself, given what is arising?*

In noticing the deeply engrained patterns underlying your relational history, you can put new possibilities on the map for doing it differently. By intentionally engaging in new behaviors, you can even move towards forming securely attached relationships with your loved ones and offer yourself the care you did not get to receive as a child.

The first step to healing these multigenerational wounds and shifting your relational patterns is cultivating the capacity to identify when your anxiety/avoid trigger is pulled. Sometimes this first step requires a lot of patience with yourself, and a lot of do-overs when you get sucked into habitual patterns of reacting or spiraling. But be gentle and kind, as best you can. You can stop the spiral at any point by shifting your attention to an anchor in the present moment and giving yourself permission to feel what you are feeling.

Once you notice you are triggered, you can now pause and anchor your attention in your body, or with another resource in the present moment, such as sound or the breath. In the space you create by taking one full breath, you can down-regulate the amygdala and bring the pre-frontal cortex back online, so that you have the capacity to choose a different response. The more you practice doing this in moments of relative safety and stability, the stronger your mental fitness becomes, and the more available it will be when life becomes challenging or overwhelming.

Once you understand what your triggers are, you can start to work with your relationship to them. There may be many years' worth of neural pathways built in this direction, and even more protective strategies guarding the gates that were once essential for survival. These barriers are there for a good reason and must not be smashed with a sledgehammer. Rather, the things we did to survive in a hostile environment must be acknowledged and honored for the wisdom they represent and for how they kept us safe when we needed them most.

With somatic awareness and a spirit of engaged curiosity in your own experience, it is also possible to revisit developmental tasks you did not get to complete along the way, and to add information to your system that you did not have back when you decided how the world works and your place within it. By acknowledging where you are wounded, and what your resulting relational tendencies are, you can then engage in appropriate practices to alchemize your pain and turn poison into medicine.

Healing generational trauma and securely attaching to a partner are not transformations that occur overnight. But you can start right now by recommitting to your own wellbeing, by carving out time for nourishing activities, and by scheduling intentional time daily to regulate and ground attention in the present moment.

Building Security in Relationships

Security in relationship can't be forced, and if you are compromising your own worthiness or boundaries to try to establish security with someone else, you'll bleed yourself dry. First, you must cultivate radical self-love, and a sense of security within your own being. You can take proactive steps towards secure attachment in any relationship (including your relationship to yourself) by:

- Choosing when to make yourself available to them and to meeting their needs. Communicating clearly when you are not available to meet their needs.
- Asking for help when you need it, and offering help only when you have capacity.
- Validating their feelings without trying to fix them or make them go away, and sharing your feelings from your own direct, felt, present moment experience.
- Making space for healthy expression and modeling authentic, non-violent communication by making requests.
- Getting involved in their interests and inviting them to join you in your own activities when it does not compromise your need for autonomy.
- Being curious about their inner life while also actively tending to your own. Being aware of your heart's electromagnetic field and the impact of your own regulation/dysregulation on others.
- Balancing time simply being together with time spent with yourself.
- Connecting in the present moment through play, somatic awareness exercises, mindfulness, movement, and music.
- Setting clear boundaries around your own needs and modeling self-care. Your emotional wellbeing is your responsibility, not theirs.
- Honoring the wisdom of your nervous system and taking the time to pause and discern whether threats are perceived or acute in the present moment before reacting.

Journal Prompt: Rewrite the story of your mother's pregnancy and your birth from the perspective of your higher self, offering yourself the welcoming into the world that you did not get to receive.

Chapter 9: Self-Love Matters

My friend, we'll call her Laura, was ready to give up on herself when she texted me pictures of the bruises on her neck where her abuser choked her.

"It's my fault because I keep going back," she wrote. "I'm in a trauma bond. I know it sounds crazy, but I miss him so much when he's gone, I end up answering his call and giving him another chance because I wish so badly that he would actually change... I don't tell anyone because I KNOW it's up to me to stop it for good. And it's something broken in me that can't help but to go back... I started it by being avoidant."

Reading her message left me dumbstruck. First, Laura is an amazing woman. She is kind, driven, and has absolutely crushed being a young, single mother facing all of life's hardships. Second, I have such a high opinion of her that I simply couldn't comprehend that she didn't have the same sense of value for herself. Once I recovered my senses and my rage cleared enough to respond to her, I peppered her with a string of affirmations of her worth and beauty, and strong (very strong) encouragement to set some boundaries, stay the f--- away from that bastard, and call the police.

I also wrote, "being avoidant is NOT an excuse for someone to assault you physically or emotionally. You are *so* worthy of safety and care, and you deserve relationships that lift you up and make you feel like the best version of yourself. The version that I see. You are so lovable. Please say that to yourself until you believe it."

The next day, Laura sent me this message: "I realized a simple truth: He expresses and acts on every bit of self-hatred I have for myself. If I want to be free from this, I need to truly believe and accept that I deserve better. And maybe deep, deep down I do believe that but something evil is convincing me that this is exactly what I deserve. He asked me sincerely yesterday if I really think I deserve someone soft and gentle with me. I said yes and he laughed so hard. I don't think either of us believed me."

Again, reading this shattered my heart. I knew she would not be able to set an effective boundary with him unless *she* believed that she was worthy of safety and care. She was right. Her self-hatred was keeping the door open to being abused. By not believing that she deserved love that was "soft and gentle," she had continued the cycle of abuse with her self-deprecating thoughts.

Fortunately, she reached out to me for help, and I responded with enough ferocious love for both of us. My outpouring of care finally convinced her she did indeed have the right to set boundaries and to be respected and protected. In finding the courage to tell me, she was able to take a crucial step in stopping the cycle – recognizing that her inner dialogue was enabling her abuser.

Awareness is the first step to breaking any pattern and thankfully, she had noticed what was happening. Now, she could slow down her impulsive thoughts and reactions, regulate her nervous system, and choose to respond differently to his attacks. She could defend herself best by believing she was worth defending.

It did take a few weeks for her to stop inviting him over and put an end to the violence for good. During that time, she told a few other friends about the situation, and received a flood of love, support, and righteous outrage. Her community had her back, and they were ready to protect her, however they could. Then one day, he slapped her and spit on her and she finally had enough. Her support system was in place, with a small army of strong men ready to show up at moment's notice, and they did. He was arrested and charged, and a restraining order put in place.

In the end, receiving the external messages of love from her friends gave her the strength to finally believe in her own worthiness, stand up for herself, and put an end to the cycle of violence. She recognized her patterning from early attachment wounds, and months later she still noticed temptation and her tendency to give in to her cravings for closeness. But with her growing awareness and support from friends, she was able to finally love herself more than her addiction to the abuser and to stop herself from contacting him.

Creating a Container of Care: Self-Talk

Our language matters. When we talk to ourselves in a way that disregards our rights to peace and safety, when we don't believe deep within that we are worthy of care and kindness and attention, this can get played out in our relationships. This becomes how others relate to us as well because we carry that belief system with us into our interactions and conversations.

It might be subtle, and we may not outwardly express these things, but our self-talk can show up in the embodied way that we hold ourselves, in how we care or don't care for ourselves, and in the way that we may or may not stand up for ourselves when we're under the threat of physical or emotional attack.

So many of us as very young children experience wounds to our belonging and threats to our worthiness that become a part of how we relate to being alive. Our inner dialogue and our thoughts impact our behaviors and emotions, even when they aren't based in fact. Making time and space for yourself and creating a container of care for yourself is an essential boundary that most people-pleasers and codependents struggle to create.

Sometimes we need help from an outside source to create this new way of talking to ourselves. Not all of us have a group of resourced, strong, mentally healthy friends who have the skills to bring us back from the brink, and it may be supportive to seek help from a therapist or crisis hotline. Needing help doesn't make you crazy, in fact asking for it takes courage and is an act of strength and loving kindness that can make all the difference.

Here's the thing about therapy: It's *all* about creating healthy boundaries. The therapy office is meant to be a place where intentional boundaries and clear guidelines can facilitate a deepening into inner experience. This is done in professional settings through the establishment of a "container": the intake form and confidentiality agreement, the therapeutic relationship, the physical space and layout of the office, the licensure and training of the therapist, the fixed timeframe of the session, and the resourcing and nervous system regulation that the therapist must commit to in their daily life outside of the session. With a clear container, you can let down your guard, connect, trust, open up, and release big feelings that have been tucked away in dark corners, festering, and crying out for attention.

All these things brought together with an individual who is caring, curious, and non-judgmental, can offer the opportunity to be held in our pain, and witnessed, and heard. These therapeutic boundaries provide the foundation for tremendous personal and relational healing. If you can find a good therapist and manage all the logistics of getting to their office, a few sessions can transform your inner landscape and change your life.

However, if you can't carve out the time, find a licensed professional you align with, or pay for the sessions, it is still possible to offer yourself time, space, and boundaries within which you can navigate big emotions and curate an inner landscape that is nurturing, caring, and kind.

All on your own, you can cultivate an internal environment of care by offering yourself time spent looking inward with an attitude of kindness, not allowing yourself to be influenced by negative thought patterns, and by regularly tending to what arises using the practices and exercises offered throughout this book.

So, take a moment here, and consider, how do you talk to yourself? Would you talk to a friend the same way? What would it be like to relate to yourself with respect and unconditional positive regard? Critical self-talk is extremely common in our achievement-based culture, and if we wish to repair our relationship to ourselves, we must start setting boundaries around our inner dialogue and create a therapeutic container around the language we use to talk to ourselves.

It's quite common to bully ourselves much worse than we ever would to anyone else. As Laura experienced, saying awful things inwardly can make them play out in our lives. Every time I catch my daughter or one of her friends saying something like "I'm so stupid," or "I suck at math," or "I'm always messing everything up," I respond right away with, "Hey! Don't talk about my friend that way." This usually gets a laugh that turns into a sad smile of realization. If I'm feeling pushy, I might encourage them to say three nice things about themselves before I let them off the hook.

Loving Kindness

One way to transform your inner landscape is to practice saying kind things to yourself, even if it feels awkward at first. When you intentionally offer yourself kind phrases, this builds new neural pathways. The more you travel these pathways, the more open and automatic they become. Rather than watering the weeds in your garden, you can focus your attention on the flowers and plants you want to thrive.

The first time you do the following exercise, I recommend setting aside five minutes or more to turn your attention inward and marinate in your own kindness. This creates a container, just like a therapy session, so that you can notice what it is like to speak this way to yourself and bring care to any resistance that arises. The more familiar you become with these phrases, the more time you can spend intentionally offering yourself loving kindness, and the more easily you can offer them to yourself anytime you catch self-critical thoughts arising, even in moments that are very busy and filled with movement and noise.

Sometimes, loving kindness phrases can be a very unfamiliar way of talking to yourself, and it may take a few rounds of practicing these phrases before they start to feel comfortable. It may be helpful to imagine yourself as a small child, or to place a photograph of yourself where you can see it during this practice. Remember, if what arises in your practice is difficult, or uncomfortable, you can use this as information and to ask yourself, *what can I do to care for myself, given what is arising?*

The first time you do this exercise, I recommend you use the 9-minute downloadable recording available at fierceboundaries.com.

Exercise 9.1: Loving Kindness for Yourself

Settle into a comfortable position. You can do this practice seated or lying down. Let your eyes close, if that feels comfortable, and take a few deep breaths. Allow yourself to settle into your body and into the present moment. With each inhale, bring new oxygen into the body, and with each exhale, invite any unnecessary stress you might be holding to flow out of your body with the breath.

Bring the full focus of attention to the area of the heart. If it feels supportive, you can put one or both hands over your heart. Feel the gentle touch of your hands, and the sensations of where your hands make contact. Let this be a reminder that you are not just bringing loving awareness to your experience and holding yourself, but you are also being held in your own awareness *and* being loved by your higher self.

As you sit here in this gesture of care and intention, start to bring to mind an image of yourself, either as you are now or as a child, or at some time in your life when you really needed kindness and compassion.

Once you have a sense of yourself in your mind's eye, bring this image into the area of your heart, kind of like tucking yourself into a bed made of loving awareness. You can repeat the following phrases silently or out loud, offering them just as you might whisper kind wishes into the ear of someone you truly love.

May I be safe.

May I be peaceful.

May I be protected from harm.

May I be free from worry.

May I be happy.

May I be healthy.

May I live with ease.

May I be free from enmity. May no hatred fill my heart.

Notice what it's like to receive these wishes of kindness. It's okay if it feels awkward or challenging. As best you can, bring curiosity and a spirit of inquiry to your experience. There is no need to "get it right" in this practice, rather sending kindness to the part of yourself that wants to get it right *is* the practice.

Now, return your attention to the sensations of the breath, coming and going in the body. Breathe in and breathe out, knowing that you are nourishing yourself with each breath, and with these wishes for kindness, compassion, and acceptance of yourself, just as you are.

Reflection What did you notice as you sent kind wishes to yourself? What was challenging? How did you meet these challenges as they arose? What do you notice now as you reflect upon this practice? How might you build intentional loving kindness for yourself into your day-to-day self-talk?

Take it Slow

Before embarking upon the practices in this next section, it is important to have a solid foundation of attentional control, anchors for attention, and resources established that have a quality of safety and invite regulation. If you need to go back and review the practices in previous chapters or prepare for this work by doing an awareness of breath practice, I strongly encourage you to do so.

Some of the practices in this chapter will invite you to recall a challenging event or communication. As best you can, to avoid re-traumatization, start by working with experiences that are manageable and don't overwhelm you. If you notice that you are becoming dysregulated, immediately take a step back from these exercises and take some time to get grounded before continuing. In many of these exercises, *the content of your memory or story is less important than the felt experience of it in your body.* If you find yourself becoming enmeshed in a series of thoughts, caught up in a terrifying narrative, or as if you are no longer in the driver's seat of your attention, it's okay to stop practicing and to resource yourself. Taking care of yourself when you get overwhelmed in practice *is the practice.* This might look like:

- Offering yourself a caring gesture (hands on heart, self-hug, holding a pillow)
- Opening the eyes and focusing your attention on an external anchor (like a tree outside of your window or a stone held in the hand)
- Moving the body (swaying side to side, standing and stretching, walking, shaking, or sweeping energy away from the body)
- Switching to a different practice that you already know to be safe and resourcing for you.
- Single tasking (sweep the floor, tidy your office, respond to one email)
- Talk to a friend.
- Change your location (step outside, take a walk, go into another room, visit a friend)

- Drink a glass of water or a cup of tea, let yourself savor it.
- Enjoy a favorite snack.
- Have a laugh (ask someone to tell you a joke, watch a funny movie, and read a lighthearted story)
- What other practices do you already use to take care of yourself when difficulty arises?

Sometimes, when we start to open our awareness to our inner experience, we might suddenly become aware of a deeply wounded relationship to ourselves. It may seem like there is more pain than there was before we practiced, but we are simply becoming aware of the pain that was already there. We can suddenly become aware of extreme exhaustion, grief, or a deficit of care and a loneliness and hurt that has built up over many years, or we may become overwhelmed by emotions and memories that we have contained since childhood. In the Mindful Self-Compassion program, developed by Dr. Kristin Neff and Chris Germer[16], this phenomenon is known as backdraft, "a firefighting term that describes what happens when a door in a burning house is opened — oxygen goes in and flames rush out. A similar process can occur when we open the door of our hearts — love goes in, and old pain comes out." If you become overwhelmed by difficult emotions, the most compassionate response may be to pull back temporarily and engage in more familiar, day-to-day acts of self-care.

Take it slow, and build gradually towards deepening your inner awareness, giving yourself the time to resource regularly. It may be helpful to imagine you are standing on a lakeshore, or on a sandy beach in front of a large body of water. Rather than plunging straight into the deep end, enter into this territory slowly, by just dipping a toe in at the edge and testing the temperature of the water. Make sure you stay close enough to the shore that if you suddenly notice a storm brewing or a sea monster swimming nearby that you can calmly return to safety. Over time, and with regular practice, your tools and strength for navigating rough seas will increase.

This is a skill called "**pendulation**," commonly used in therapeutic trauma work. As you turn towards difficulty, return frequently to a home base of resource and groundedness. This helps your brain learn that you are no longer in the moment of threat, but that you are investigating and bringing awareness to the imprint of threat from a place of safety in the present moment.

Though many of us are habituated to getting as much done in as little time as possible, self-compassion is different. There is nothing to be gained by rushing through this portion of the work. It is a lifestyle change that takes repeated practice and commitment to your own wellbeing. Much like a garden, the seeds of self-compassion must be regularly watered, and the weeds pulled. It's useless to do all that work in one day and then ignore the garden for months. Instead, it's better to pull a few weeds each day, and take great care to choose which seeds you plant and water.

Luckily, you can plant seeds of self-compassion everywhere you go, without having to set aside time on your calendar. Each time you catch yourself having a self-critical thought, this can be a moment of self-compassion. Just like we teach children to reframe their thinking around a growth mindset, you can do the same for yourself. The phrases below are ones I suggest you keep in your back pocket, as a replacement for self-criticism. You can even write them on sticky notes and post them around the house or in your office where you are likely to see them frequently.

You are enough.
You are worthy of love.
You deserve rest.
You are doing the best you can.
You are strong.

You deserve care and attention.

It's okay to ask for help.

You are making a difference.

Self-Compassion

For the following self-compassion meditation, you'll be invited to work with a situation or scenario that has some difficulty for you in your life. This might be a situation of personal challenge, like chronic pain in the body, or injury, or illness. It could be an interpersonal situation, some conflict or relationship challenge in your life, perhaps a difficult person, or a difficult communication. Or, it could be a larger societal condition, some situation that impacts you in a way that is challenging.

If this is your first time doing a practice like this, it's very important to begin with something small and manageable, so avoid choosing the most difficult situation or a situation in which you are likely to become overwhelmed or dysregulated. If you do become overwhelmed, it's okay to stop practicing, to bring attention back to an anchor in the present moment and to use your orienting skills to re-establish safety in the body. It's *not* useful to plunge ahead into dangerous waters without a lifeboat.

The first time you do the following exercise, I recommend you access the 9-minute downloadable recording at fierceboundaries.com. Abbreviated instructions are included below.

Exercise 9.2: Soften, Soothe, Allow

Once you have chosen a situation that is manageable, and have this situation in your awareness, **bring attention to an anchor** of your choosing, such as the breath, sound, or the sensations of gravity in the body. Spend a few moments, marinating here, memorizing this resource as a safe place for your attention.

Let the scenario play out in your awareness as you bring investigative curiosity to how this experience is alive in the body. See if you can identify the emotion you are feeling. Is it sadness? Grief? Anger? Frustration? Give yourself permission to get curious about this emotion. What's here? What are the **sensations in the body** that accompany this emotion?

As you explore these sensations, start to **soften** around them. You might even choose to place a hand on the heart, or embrace yourself, letting these feelings soften. You could even imagine that as you inhale, you are breathing new oxygen into this area of difficulty, and that as you exhale, you are releasing what is no longer useful, and softening around the sensations a little bit more.

Now, bring a quality of **soothing** to them, as if you are comforting a child, and acknowledge that this is a wounded place. This hurts. You can offer some words to yourself, like "I'm right here with you. I see you. I've got you. This is really hard." It may be supportive now, if you haven't already, to bring a hand to your heart or to the belly, and to offer yourself a gesture of holding and being held.

With the hands on the body, let the hands say to the heart "it's okay to feel this way. Your feelings are real. These feelings belong." Really **allow** yourself to have this experience. Let the breath expand into these sensations, inviting just a little bit more space for them.

When you are ready, release this experience of difficulty as the object of attention, and return attention back to the sensations of gravity in the body. Become aware of the pressure where the body touches a surface, and notice the support that's available from the ground, or the chair, or the cushion. See if you can allow yourself to be held here, in **loving awareness**, just for a moment longer.

Shift attention back to the breath, giving yourself permission to take three full breaths all the way in and out, fully attending to the movement of air into and out of the body.

Reflection: What did you notice as you brought the difficult situation into your awareness? What emotions showed up and how did you meet them? What do you notice now as you reflect upon this practice? How might you build intentional pauses to soften, soothe, and allow into your workday?

If the practices in this chapter have been helpful for you, I highly recommend you check out the vast body of work associated with Mindful Self Compassion. Kristin Neff has numerous free downloadable meditations, and many books, courses, and online resources. I personally have benefitted tremendously from using the above "Soften, Soothe, Allow" meditation during moments of emotional upheaval. I find this practice really supports me in making space for my emotions and for bringing tenderness and care to my experience. You may wish to return to this practice as we move forward into deepening our relationship with our body wisdom and working skillfully with challenges.

Chapter 10: Curate Your Mental
Real Estate

One Wednesday in April, a year before the Covid-19 Pandemic and four days before the 20th anniversary of the Columbine High School shooting, a "credible threat of gun violence" shut down schools across the Denver Metro area. Teachers, parents, and students at home dealt with high levels of fear, stress, and anxiety as police cruisers patrolled empty school parking lots.

Across the state, worried parents scrambled to make plans for their kids and to explain the situation in a way that made sense, with their hearts pounding and their minds racing with thoughts of *what am I going to do? Is my kid safe? How can this be happening again?*

Our nervous systems are designed to attune to each other, and we have **mirror neurons** that give us a sense in our own bodies of what others are feeling. This means that when people around us are stressed, anxious, and afraid, we will pick up on these emotions and experience them in our own systems. In this situation, the very real and present danger was the contagion of the fear itself. If you were unfortunate enough to be on the roads that day, navigating a churning sea of panic, you saw a clear example of this phenomenon in action.

But the blaring horns and fierce gestures made sense, given that most people on the roads that day were driving in terror. Along the way to wherever they were unexpectedly going, many of them were also trying to explain to their frightened children that there might be a woman coming to their school with a gun who wanted to kill them, all while buried in a flurry of texts and arrangements and cancelled appointments, with the whole state at threat level orange.

The cause of the alarm was a depressed and mentally unstable 18-year-old woman named Sol País. The news[17] reported that she was "infatuated with Columbine," had purchased a pump action shotgun, and had flown to Colorado after making verbal threats in Miami. The FBI searched for her as panic gripped the state. In a sad and lonely turn of events, the young, distressed woman was found dead from a gunshot wound in the mountains. The autopsy report indicated she had taken her own life the day before the lockdown.

In hindsight, though the students were not in real danger that day, the fear itself was very real, and it had consequences. Worry rippled through millions of minds, as people spent their hours of chaos, helplessness, and uncertainty wondering *am I safe? What should I do to protect my kids? Should we start a revolution and take to the streets? What if there is a sniper? Will schools ever be safe again?* We are very good at this kind of worst-case scenario thinking because we have been well trained by the news media, active shooter drills, and our own habits of catastrophizing that only make it worse.

Remember, when we are in a fear response, the nervous system lights up and mobilizes to defend against an attack. The amygdala dumps cortisol into the system, the body prepares for fight or flight, and the prefrontal cortex goes off-line, taking with it our decision-making and executive-functioning capabilities. When we are in this mode, we are prone to reactivity and poor decision-making. We may be irritable or clumsy, or off-balance and injury prone. Our relationships suffer and we can do and say things we later regret, like cursing at the grocery store clerk, yelling at our children, or giving our neighbor the finger.

If we let them, our thoughts can run away with us and take us for a terrifying ride.

In the throes of my divorce, my thoughts were my nemesis. Because my ex constantly threatened self-harm and lashed out with bitter accusations, I was always ruminating, tense, or on guard, thinking about the right thing to say and worried about the worst-case scenario. He had penetrated every corner of my mind and taken up residency there. Even though he was no longer living in my house, and I rarely saw him, his threats were everywhere, all the time, lurking inside of every waking moment.

I was so primed for fear that even the gentle buzz of a text message arriving on my phone made me jump. It was difficult to sleep. I became short-tempered and snappy with my daughter. I coped by numbing with alcohol and drugs. The fear circled around on itself, and my thoughts sent me plummeting down the rabbit hole of terror.

Despite my meditation practice and applying the attentional training exercises from the first half of this book, thoughts of him haunted me like a hungry ghost. I was trapped in a thought spiral, hooked in a cycle of fear and reactivity.

As any parent who kept their kid home from school that day or child who has ever been awake at night, hiding under the covers and scared of what lurks in the shadows, can tell you – the monsters are real. They sneak up on us when we're alone, when we have our backs turned, and when we leave our closet doors cracked open. They live in the untended recesses of our mind, and they feed on our fear and insecurity.

The monsters are real because our fear is real, and they won't go away until we turn on the light and have a good look around, or crawl into bed next to someone else. Even when the fear isn't based in what is visible or tangible in the present moment, if we believe we have a good reason to be scared, a threat to our safety or belonging can take hold of us at any hour of the day or night. And the more we focus on the shape of the shadows, the larger they loom.

Acknowledge that the Fear is Real

The next time you find yourself terrified of something you can't see, or hijacked into worrying about a relationship with someone who isn't even in the room with you, see if you can get back in the driver's seat of your own experience and reclaim your mental real estate. You can do this by practicing the following skill:

Exercise 10.1: Name It to Tame It

Slow down and **notice** that you feel fear (or any other emotion) and let yourself experience it, rather than ignoring it or trying to make it go away. Say to yourself, "fear is present." Acknowledge that the feeling is real.

Name the sensations (racing heart, tight jaw, clenched fists, heat in your face). From this perspective of the witness, check out what fear really does in your mind and body. Get to know it.

How do you know you are afraid? What does fear want you to know? Is

---

this a thought or a fact?

Now breathe. Take three full breaths, all the way in and all the way out. Expand your awareness to include the breath, body, and the space and people or situation around you. Look around the room and identify the exits and any windows. Feel your feet on the floor. Feel the shape and weight of your hands. Notice the movement of air across your skin.

Proceed with awareness.

Reflection: How can you best care for yourself, given what showed up during that exercise?

Without letting it overrun our nervous systems, we must accept that we are living in times of extreme fear and reactivity, hopelessness, coping, addiction, depression, suicide, the loss of the value of human connection, and the destruction of the planet itself. The increase of isolation, the lack of healthy coping skills, and the resulting skyrocketing rates of mental illness have created an environment in which we are chronically at war with each other and within ourselves. The threat of someone coming into your child's school with a gun, and deliberately hurting your precious little ones, is the worst kind of violence imaginable. The fear is real. You're not alone. And we do have to *do* something. Our children's lives and their well-being are in danger every day.

Slowing down and practicing somatic awareness isn't a failure to act. Rather, it gives us an invitation to pause, breathe, notice what is present, and to skillfully choose a response. **We get to choose how to *be* in the face of the fear.**

Naming our emotions and thoughts gives us the opportunity to acknowledge them, to turn towards difficulty, and to embrace challenges with curiosity and care. But can we really hold the threat of our children being unsafe at school with kindness? Yes. We can be kind to ourselves and honor that our fear is real. We can model skillful coping even in the face of distress. We can reclaim our mental real estate by intentionally shifting our attention away from catastrophic thoughts and to our present moment experience. By acknowledging that we are facing extreme difficulty, we can then bring awareness to our experience and choose a wise, skillful response instead of an automatic reaction.

Fear is in the air, and our nervous systems are designed to pick up on the nervous systems of those around us. This is not something to be taken lightly. If you become reactive in the face of a threat, no matter how big or small it may seem, see if you can check yourself. Know that this reactivity is normal, and **you deserve to feel angry right now.**

I challenge you to follow the path of the peaceful warrior and to remain calm in the face of distress. We are on the battlefield of hearts and minds, and lives are at stake. You must be calm, cool, collected, and able to think clearly when you are needed. The best thing you can do for yourself in the face of this threat, is to tend to yourself, to care for those around you, and to radiate peace, love, kindness, and compassion in all directions, as best you can.

Anger is made of energy for change, and if we can channel our emotions towards what is useful, kind, and skillful, rather than raging, panicking, and flipping each other off in traffic, we can use our anger to act wisely. Don't waste it by letting it paralyze you or taking it out on others who are just as angry and afraid as you are. Breathe and wake up and practice focused attention so that when the time comes you can hear the call to action and be the change you wish to see in the world.

For this moment, take the time to breathe the air. Feel your skin. Feel your feet on the ground. Taste your food. Really let yourself experience it. Slow down. Do what moves you. Let it out. Follow your heart. Express your frustration in ways that matter. Paint, create, dance, move, write, love, feel, explore, spend time in nature with your kids. Run. Laugh. Play. Keep going. Come back to the present moment again and again. It is all we really have.

And when you get lost, and your mind is overrun with all the suffering and violence in the world, ask yourself, *how do I choose to live in these troubled times?*

Thoughts Aren't Facts

Many of us have core wounds of not-belonging or beliefs about our worthiness that are formed in environments devastated by ongoing relational conflict and alienation, and these beliefs are magnified by the proliferation of fear-based thinking in advertising and news media. Setting boundaries around our thoughts and reclaiming our mental real estate can give us back power in a capitalist society that profits when we're unaware, divided, fearful, and powerless.

Messages that we are in danger or not good enough are so pervasive in our culture, it's no wonder that many of us live in a state of chronic fear and hyperarousal and choose retail therapy, hyper-productivity, intoxication, and isolation over the risk of rejection. We are praised for our self-sufficiency and discouraged from burdening anyone else with our troubles (because they already have enough to deal with). We are dismissive of our own needs for rest, loving touch, and play. We are valued for our professionalism when we suppress our emotions, and celebrated for conforming, even when it strips us of our authenticity and humanness.

Our thoughts and fears are in the driver's seat, taking up all the available space in our minds, looping on repeat and running our lives. And we only stay on this hamster wheel and follow this social contract because that's what everyone else is doing and we *think* we must do it too, so that we can belong and stay safe.

Here's the thing. *We don't have to believe everything we think, and our thoughts aren't always true.* But we can also make things true by believing them. We create our reality with our thoughts, and even seemingly innocuous phrases, such as "I *need* a drink," or "watching tv is the *only* way I can relax," or "I don't have time for self-care," can make those statements come to life.

We are never taught the skill of **metacognition** (bringing awareness to thoughts) in school and as a result we can easily become trapped in habitual cycles of maladaptive coping that clutter our minds and dump even more stress into our dysregulated systems. Many of us manage our exhaustion by turning off our awareness and our knowing and tuning out. We treat the symptoms of our stress and overwhelm with quick-fixes that dampen the noise and take us even further away from ourselves — numbing, dissociating, ignoring, and avoiding with drugs, alcohol, binge-watching, over-eating, and scrolling social media. The addictive dopamine hits and temporary bursts of pleasure that we get from "scratching the itch" or giving in to a craving are merely Band-Aids that we slap over the gaping wounds of our not-belonging.

Skill: Metacognition

Metacognition is the ability to notice thoughts arising and passing, and to understand your thought patterns and triggers. This involves being able to identify the quality of a thought, it's impact on emotions and behaviors, and to discern which thoughts are true and require action, and which do not.

The following is an exercise used in MBCT and MBSR that can help strengthen the skill of metacognition. Becoming aware of how your mind works gives you the opportunity to familiarize yourself with the thoughts that may not be true, and how to shift your attention with intention to avoid becoming enmeshed in thoughts. This is an essential skill to develop in the landscape of setting boundaries so that you can **disengage from unhelpful and untrue thoughts**, shift your attention to what is real and true in the present moment, and avoid participating in toxic relationship and thought patterns.

Awareness of thoughts involves noticing them as they arise and pass, without becoming attached to them, or wrapped up in the content of the story. For this exercise, see if you can rest in the perspective of the observer, much like a passenger on a train platform, watching the thought train pull into the station, pause, and continue on its way, without climbing on board.

If you do get taken for a ride and become wrapped up or hooked on one train of thought, simply notice this, and with gentleness and care, guide your attention back to the platform. You can practice this for just a few moments at a time, or for longer periods of sitting, both of which can help you cultivate the capacity to let go of rumination, self-criticism, and habitual patterns of reactivity. The first time you do this exercise, I encourage you to use the 13-minute downloadable recording available at fierceboundaries.com.

Exercise 10.2: Awareness of Thoughts

Start by establishing a resting place in the present moment using an anchor that is familiar to you, such as the breath, sound, or sensations of gravity in the body. Then, when you feel like attention has settled, bring your awareness to any thoughts that are coming and going. If there are no thoughts, that's okay too. Simply notice whatever is here to be noticed.

If it is supportive, you can use the metaphor of your mind as the sky and the thoughts as clouds. Alternatively, you can imagine you are standing on a train platform, watching the trains of thought arrive and depart from the station. Notice the quality of thoughts. Are they fast, slow, racing, troubling, or jumpy? Or maybe there is one train of thought that is especially sticky or magnetic. See if you can notice this, without becoming absorbed in the content of the thoughts.

It can be helpful to use a gentle noting practice, where you label the types of thoughts that are coming and going. For example, you might say to yourself, "thoughts about work," or "thoughts about money." Using this noting practice can be helpful for keeping yourself on the platform and avoiding getting carried away by story about the thoughts.

Remember, that the goal here isn't to clear your mind, or to make thoughts stop or go away. Your job is to simply notice thoughts as they arise and observe them as they pass through experience. If this is challenging, know that this is completely normal. See if you can just track one thought, all the way from its inception, as it blossoms into awareness, and fades. How do you notice the beginning of a thought, and the end of a thought?

When you practice in this way, observing thoughts and your relationship to them, you not only become stronger in conducting your attention, but you also get to know how your mind works. This can be very helpful in working with habitual patterns and chronic reactivity. So, take a moment here, before completing this practice, and congratulate yourself for tending to yourself in this way.

When you are ready, go ahead and bring attention back to the breath for a few moments before letting go of this exercise, and bringing this moment-to-moment attention into the next moments of your day.

Reflection: What did you notice as you brought your attention to your thoughts? Was it easy or challenging to watch thoughts without getting wrapped up in them? Did you have any thoughts that were familiar? Did you have any thoughts that weren't necessarily true?

The Language of Thoughts and Feelings

Culture and popular language that are used to name and process your emotions have an impact on how you experience them. For example, if you're feeling angry, you might say "I am so angry!"

Then, an expected response from a friend might be, "Why? What happened?"

This question begins a cognitive process of trying to figure out the root of the anger in your thoughts, and inherently takes you swirling into the past as you run down the rabbit hole of who did what, and how dare he, and I can't believe she said that. Or, what an awful person he is for making you feel this way.

Additionally, when you use the words "I *am* angry," you are identifying yourself as anger. Anger has control over your entire experience, and it is what you *are*. These linguistic and thought patterns are deeply embedded in our culture, which is one of the reasons we (as a society) can so easily be overtaken by big feelings. The problem with the English language way of identifying ourselves as the emotion itself is that the words we use drive us into our thoughts, and away from the felt experience of the emotion in the body.

Neuroscience and MRI research by Dr. Jill Bolte Taylor, Ph.D. has demonstrated that emotions move through experience like waves lasting about 90 seconds[18]. They come, they peak, and if we allow ourselves to acknowledge them and feel them, they subside. If we experience an emotion for more than a few minutes, we are likely avoiding it or re-triggering it with our thoughts.

"Something happens in the external world, and chemicals are flushed through your body which puts it on full alert. For those chemicals to totally flush out of the body, it takes less than 90 seconds. This means that for 90 seconds you can watch the process happening, you can feel it happening, and then you can watch it go away. After that, if you continue to feel fear, anger, and so on, you need to look at the thoughts that you're thinking that are re-stimulating the circuitry that is resulting in you having this physiological reaction, over and over again."

-Dr. Jill Bolte Taylor, Ph.D.

What if rather than trying to figure out why we feel the way we feel, we simply allowed ourselves to feel that way? By bringing somatic awareness to the experience of an emotion, allowing yourself to *feel* what you are feeling, and investigating how it is showing up in the body in the present moment, you can step back into the driver's seat of your experience. **You can *feel* your feelings** and allow them to arise and pass, **rather than *think* your feelings**, and swirl into a black hole of rumination. This is the essential skill behind the name it to tame it exercise offered earlier in this chapter.

In addition, remembering that we can speak things into truth, it can be helpful to change the language we use to talk about our emotional experiences. Most other cultures have linguistic distinctions that allow for the temporary nature of emotions. In Irish, the construction would be *tá brón orm*, meaning "sadness is on me," rather than "I am sad." Sadness is acknowledged, but it does not define who you are as a person.

In Spanish, there are two different words that translate to "I am." One of them, *"soy,"* is used for permanent conditions, such as *"soy una mujer,"* or "I am a woman." The other, *"estoy,"* is used for impermanent conditions, such as *"estoy triste,"* or "I am sad (just for right now)." Embedded within the language is the implication that the emotion of sadness is not permanent. On the other hand, if I said, *"soy triste,"* it would translate to "I am a sad person, always and forever."

When I teach this concept, I start by drawing two circles on the whiteboard that represent the "self" (see diagram on opposite page). Above the first circle, I write the words "I am angry." Then I put the word "ANGRY" in the middle of the circle in all caps and draw some lines radiating outward to show that when we use this phrase to identify our emotion, we are hijacked by the emotion. It takes over our entire experience.

Above the second circle, I write the words "Anger is Present." Then I have students share out body sensations that go with anger. I ask, "what in your felt, present moment experience tells you that you are angry?" Inside the circle, I write their responses, such as "heart racing, chest tightening, hands in fists, impulse to yell/hit, jaw clenched, ears pounding, etc." Often, the list of physical sensations quickly fills up the circle.

You can play with the language to see what works for you. You might use "anger is here," or "anger is present," or "I feel angry." Any of these constructions give you the opportunity to ask that next question, "how do I know it's anger? What sensations tell me anger is here?" In doing this, you are feeling your feelings, rather than thinking your feelings. This shifts your attention down into your body where you can disentangle your "self" from the emotion and investigate it with the tools that we have already practiced.

To take this practice even further, you can then expand your awareness to include other sensory information inside and outside the body. What do you notice in your present moment experience that is *not* anger?

If you become overwhelmed by the feeling of anger, you can intentionally shift your attention to an anchor that is stabilizing. This can help regulate your nervous system and ground you so that you can respond with all your capacities online. It can also be a way that you reclaim your mental real estate when you're hooked into rumination or overwhelmed by an emotion.

"I am angry"

Self ⟶

ANGRY

Hijacked by Emotion. The experience of anger takes over. Our brain is in survival mode, can't access PFC.

"Anger is Present"

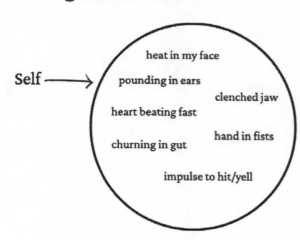

Self ⟶

heat in my face

pounding in ears

clenched jaw

heart beating fast

hand in fists

churning in gut

impulse to hit/yell

How do you notice anger in your body? FEEL your feelings (rather than THINK your feelings) to get back in the driver's seat.

Investigate/Observe:
What is here now?

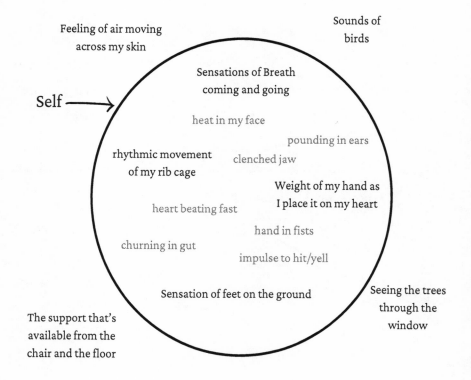

Allow yourself to <u>feel</u> what you feel. It's okay to feel this. This feeling is a part of you. What else do you notice with your senses in the present moment?

Skill: Shifting Attention Away from Triggering Stimuli

When you notice you are hooked into a thought that is not helpful or true, give it a label (thoughts about work, thoughts about not having enough money, thoughts about an argument).

Shift attention out of your thoughts and towards your felt experience in the body. What emotion is here? How do you know?

Identify other parts of your felt or sensory experience outside of that emotion. Choose one that is neutral or pleasant and bring your attention to rest here. Allow this to be an anchor.

When you get pulled back into the troublesome thought or feeling, notice that attention has shifted, and gently redirect your focus to the anchor.

Reflection: What sensations accompanied the difficult emotion? What did you notice as you brought attention to rest on an anchor that was neutral or pleasant? What do you notice now?

Tend to Your Garden: The Seeds you Water Grow

Last year, I was determined to grow a garden. In the spring I worked diligently, digging and turning soil, pushing kale seeds and beans down into the dirt with my fingers, setting up sprinklers and trellises, and clearing away a forest of weeds. I placed a bobble-head owl on the fencepost to keep the rodents away and surrounded my small beds with fine wire-mesh fencing. But in June, just as the tender sprouts were pushing through the soil, we were overrun with mosquitoes, and spending more than thirty seconds outside in the high-pitched whine was unbearable. So, I set the sprinklers on a timer and went traveling until the mosquitoes were gone.

When I returned to the garden in August, it was completely overrun with thorny thistles, cheat grass, and cockleburs. Everything edible had hardly grown, as it had all been shaded by the towering weeds and was dried out at the roots. My sprinklers had watered the weeds so much they were thriving and the vegetables I wanted to grow had been crowded out.

So, I put on thick leather gloves and a long-sleeved shirt, removed the fencing, and set to pulling the spikey, thick stalks, which required yanking and hacking and much more physical exertion than simply driving to the store to buy some kale. Beneath one patch of fuzzy grass, I was delighted to find some healthy bean plants with a handful of pods, ready for picking. Sitting there in the garden, I ate all the beans that were ready, leaving those that needed to grow a bit more hanging on the vine. I cleared the rest of the weeds around them, watered them thoroughly, and went to bed.

The next morning, I found that a midnight visitor had also discovered the newly revealed bean plants and had chomped them all down to the roots. There was nothing left but a torn away half-inch of stalk. My precious beans were gone.

It was my last attempt at gardening in this high-altitude, mosquito-ridden, rodent- and weed-infested climate. I had put dozens of hours, hundreds of dollars, and my blood, sweat, and tears into that garden, and because I did not tend it the way it needed, all I ended up with was a small handful of beans, eaten in one sitting.

Just as neural pathways are like trails cut through a jungle that require tending, the thoughts in our minds are like plants growing in a garden. If the garden of our minds is neglected and overgrown with tall thorny weeds, it can be impossible for the tender sprouts of worthiness, care, wellbeing, and self-love to get the water and sunlight they need to thrive. Not only do we need to water the seeds we wish to grow, we also must put measures in place to stop more weeds and rodents from coming into our garden and destroying what we have cultivated.

If the metaphor of the garden works for you, great. Run with it. If not, here's another one. The Chinese practice of Feng Shui is about designing the details of your environment to promote harmony, happiness, and wellbeing. It involves the intentional curation of physical spaces by organizing life experiences around a center, keeping the movement of energy balanced and in flow, furnishing the space with nourishing elements, and eliminating what is excess, stagnant, or not useful. There is truth to the saying "cluttered house, cluttered mind," and the evidence indicates that carefully designing your external spaces has a positive impact on your internal environment. Just as we can carefully select and place furniture in a room, we can become the curator of what takes up space in our minds, choose what to designate as the focal point, and get rid of what's not useful or keep it from coming into our space in the first place.

Our inner landscape is fed by what we take in, and toxic relationships, work and social pressures, visual and print media, and automatic negative thoughts can poison us. But to stop feeding our minds with poison, we must first recognize that we are doing it so that we can choose differently. Tending to our mental real estate requires practicing the skills already presented in this chapter of metacognition, intentionally changing our language around emotions, and shifting focus away from thoughts that do not serve us. But we must also take stock of our **mental diet** and practice **discernment**.

Discernment means choosing a wise response based on knowing the difference between thoughts that are true and require action, and thoughts that are not facts, that we can allow to arise and pass, without getting taken along for a ride. We can use the skill of discernment to curate a nourishing environment within our minds by setting clear boundaries around what we are willing to take in, the people with whom we surround ourselves, and the messages about our worthiness that we choose to believe.

Exercise 10.3: What Are You Taking In?

Over the course of a few days, make a list of everything you "ingest" as part of your mental diet. Include television shows, books, movies, video games, news, emails, social media, music, water cooler conversations, gossip, workplace discussions, attitudes, messages from friends, partners, parents, visual art, clutter or tidiness of your home, photographs on your fridge, etc. Let this list be exhaustive.

Using a highlighter or colored marker, circle the items on your list that are nourishing and support a mental landscape of harmony, happiness, and wellbeing. Think of these as the flowers in your garden.

Then, using a different color, cross out all the items on your list that are depleting, toxic, or unnecessary. Think of these items as the weeds.

Moving forward, focus your attention on the parts of your diet that are nourishing, watering the flowers. Look for opportunities to eliminate what is depleting, pulling the weeds. You may not be able to fully eliminate some of the depleting items, but you can choose not to water them with your attention.

Reflection: What relationship do you notice between what you have been taking in and the health of your mental garden? How might you limit your participation in activities and communications that are not nourishing your wellbeing? What nourishing activities can you engage in that can replace the depleting ones?

Chapter 11: Take Back Time

T ime is a human construct, and within the western mindset of linear time, we have become prisoners to it. Time is always running out, and we give our power away by allowing systems of control to manipulate how we "spend" our time. Our lives consist of a finite amount of time that is in scarcity and will inevitably end up not being enough. We can't get it back once it's gone, and yet we are always rushing forward into the future, with a great sense of urgency, blasting through the time that we do have on our way to something bigger and better.

Time is precious. Getting fierce around how we allocate our time each day, what we choose to attend to, and how we relate to time can add spaciousness, autonomy, and freedom to our lives. But we can only reclaim our mastery of time if we have clarity around our priorities, a willingness to invest in our future selves by acting consciously and with discernment in the present moment, and a strong "no" in our pockets.

Beware the "Time Thief"

As a mom who has attempted to co-parent peacefully with my abusive and manipulative ex, I have often experienced the sudden, rage-inducing hijacking of the time I thought I would have to engage in activities that require me to be free from the distraction of parenting responsibilities (such as writing, meditation, art, and connecting with adult friends).

It goes something like this: He says he will pick our daughter up at five p.m. and keep her for the weekend. So, we plan our day around this, turn down playdates, refrain from taking after-school trips to the pool, hold off on walking the dogs, and avoid getting started on anything that will be interrupted when he arrives. I make plans for an evening out with friends once she is gone, and to get a solid chunk of writing done the next morning.

The planned pick-up time comes and goes, and half an hour later, we are both wondering, *what happened to Dad? When is he going to be here?* I am hesitant to send a message to him because I have placed some boundaries around digital communication for reasons I'll come back to in the next chapter. So, we wait. My frustration and impatience build.

Meanwhile, my daughter settles in to her afternoon, and the excitement and positive energy she had mustered for going to her dad's begins to fizzle out. She yawns, says that she is tired, and expresses that maybe she just wants to stay home for the night so that she can relax and go to bed early. With the uncertainty of the evening growing moment by moment, I cancel my plans to go out and we move towards preparing dinner and choosing a movie to watch. Finally, an hour after he was supposed to pick her up, we get a message that he is just leaving work, 60 miles away, and plans to stop at the grocery store on the way home. He is wondering what she wants for dinner. He will probably be home around 7:30.

At this point, she is curled up with the dogs under a blanket and watching television and does not want to leave the house. "I'll just go to dad's tomorrow morning," she sighs. And the cycle continues.

It has been happening this way for years and has been a source of ongoing resentment and hostility between us since before the divorce. In the first months after we split up, when my ex was most troubled and unstable, he and I battled constantly over commitment to parenting time. Back then, I still worked as a schoolteacher, and our daughter was just a toddler. My work obligations dominated my schedule, and I was overwhelmed, under-rested, and always in need of more time to myself to regulate and recover.

There was another teacher at my school I had befriended who was also going through a divorce from a man who struggled with mental illness and dysregulation. When I shared with her my frustration that my ex frequently had to pull out of his scheduled parenting time due to instability or his lack of ability to plan effectively, she nodded with understanding. Both of us spent much of our time hungry for a break and during the time that our children were with their fathers we ended up feeling so anxious about their safety that we were unable to get the rest or give ourselves the care that we so desperately needed. We knew we needed time to ourselves to be good mothers, but we were mothers before we were anything else, and we worried about our children spending time with their mentally ill fathers, as troubled as they were.

"I will always take my children," she said, eyes blazing with the ferocity of a lioness. "Always."

In that moment, I realized that it wasn't a matter of losing *my* free time, but that my number one priority was the safety and health of my daughter. I had to *stop relying on my unreliable ex* to give me rest and space to recover myself. This is especially hard for a recovering codependent like me. If I wanted control over my life, I had to stop allowing my ex's mental health to control my schedule, take agency over my own time, and stop placing my rights to my own wellbeing in the hands of someone who did not respect them.

I had to recognize that it wasn't his responsibility to make space for my need for rest, just as it wasn't my responsibility to take on the burden of his emotional wellbeing or rescue him from his inability to commit to parenthood. I would have to find a way to tend to myself while parenting, assume that it was entirely up to me to run my own life, and to do it without depending on him to make it possible. I had to shift my perspective and my attitude. It wasn't about forcing my child onto to her unstable dad so that I could get myself back, but about shifting how I allowed myself to be in relationship to time while I was with her.

"You're right. I will always take my daughter," I committed. This commitment did not mean that I no longer sent my daughter to her dad's or had time to myself. Instead, I learned not to depend on him, and to let go of attachment to the idea that when she was with him, I would finally have "free time." I also started asking for help from my friends, which was very challenging at first, but I quickly realized that they often enjoyed supporting me. Surprisingly enough, it was okay to seek childcare and support from dependable people when I needed to schedule time for myself. The less I relied on him, the more agency I felt in my own life.

Though we still have situations that are unpredictable, and he continues to be unreliable in terms of sticking to planned schedules, both me and my daughter have made peace with this. Rather than spending our time ruminating and frustrated that he cannot show up when he says he will, we simply roll our eyes, shrug our shoulders, and move on with our day. We don't plan around when he says he will available, and though I make the most of the "free time" I do have, I never rely on him for it.

Most of all, I want my daughter to know that I am always available for her. I am her mother 100 percent of the time, regardless of her father's schedule, and she is always welcome to be with me when she needs me. I will always and forever take my daughter.

Time can only be stolen if you give it away and leave it out in the open for others to covet. It's taken me a few years to get my priorities straight and to summon the strength to get fierce with my boundaries, but now that I have, I am no longer available to be a prisoner of time nor am I available to operate at the mercy of those who are living in so much time scarcity that they cannot make time for what matters.

"Einstein Time"

Shortly after I left classroom teaching, I started working with a therapist who recommended the book *The Big Leap* by Gay Hendricks[19], within which the author posits that our relationship to time has everything to do with how we experience it. Hendricks calls our traditional way of thinking about time "Newtonian Time." With this mindset, time is in a fixed quantity and exists outside of us and is something we must go out and get. It is always in scarcity.

Time goes especially quickly when we are having fun. Hendricks writes, "an hour with your beloved feels like a minute; a minute on a hot stove feels like an hour!" Therefore, the speed at which time flies or crawls is all in our minds. This brings us to the concept of "Einstein Time." In this way of thinking about time, it's all relative. Our perception is everything. *You are where time comes from. You create time.*

Say you are running late for a meeting, and you are stuck in traffic. With a mindset of Newtonian time, stress in this situation is inevitable.

Why aren't we moving faster? My boss is going to be so mad at me. I should have left the house sooner. What's this guy's problem? Why is he pulling out in front of me? Thinking this way is loaded with regret, shame, blame, anxiety, and urgency. None of these attitudes are going to make the situation any better. In fact, "haste makes waste," and when we stress in this way, we create a negative feedback loop where now we not only are late, but we also have a system full of cortisol, adrenaline, and bitter feelings.

On the other hand, applying the principles of Einstein Time to this situation changes everything. If I am the one who creates time, then I choose how I fill my time. I may be "late" to work by someone else's schedule, but no matter how much I stress I will still be late. I chose to be late when I spend those extra minutes in bed, or savoring my coffee, lingering in the shower, and calmly dropping my daughter off at daycare. Now, instead of filling my time in the car with anxiety and worry, I can recognize that I have control of my attitude right now, shift my attention into the present moment, feel my body in space, and I can relax, enjoy my favorite music on the radio, and smile and send kind thoughts to other drivers on the road.

This shift has had a huge impact on my day-to-day mental and emotional health. Time is a human construct, and when we live grounded in the present moment and with a sense of agency over how we relate to the choices that we make, we gain the infinite and eternal freedom of Einstein time.

Skill: Be the Source of Time

Bring awareness to how you speak about time and notice whether you use scarcity language or creation language. Changing the language you use can change your relationship to time. See if you can start to shift your perspective to one of relativity in relationship to time and adopt language that makes you the source of time.

Newtonian Time sounds like:
- I don't have time…
- "Killing" or "spending" time…
- I can't wait until…
- There's never enough time…
- I can squeeze in time for…
- Time is up. We're out of time…

Einstein Time sounds like:
- I choose to *fill* my time with…
- I don't have capacity for that right now…
- I am available to make time for…
- I am not available to make time for…
- I'm looking forward to…
- I am going to carve out some time for…
- It's time to bring this activity to completion and transition…

Reflection: What shifts when you change the language you use to speak about time? How does this change how you experience the creation/scarcity of time?

Make Time for What Matters Most

In my work with educators, I regularly see the scarcity-of-time mindset adding stress to their already overwhelming jobs. The start of the school year is the beginning of the race through the list of tasks that never ends until summer break nine months later. Bells punctuate the day to mark the beginnings and endings of overly specific class start times (like 10:43). Students rush from class to class during obscenely brief passing periods (2.5 minutes in some schools), getting reprimanded when they arrive late. Teachers are under the pressure of volumes of evidence outcomes and standards and achievement-focused leadership that promotes "bell-to-bell instruction" and embodies a false urgency to get through a mountain of content in as little time as possible.

Blood pressure is high, and morale is low.

There is never enough time to get it all done with any sense of satisfaction because there is always more to do. To stay ahead of the overwhelm, teachers arrive at work early just to find a moment of focus and organization before the day dissolves into chaos. "Free periods" are used for grading and lesson planning, and after school time is used for meetings and extracurriculars. By the time they arrive home at the end of the day, often toting a bag full of papers to grade, they are too exhausted to work out, or make a healthy dinner, or devote undivided attention to their own children. Then, the stress of all the work they didn't get done or ruminating about the situations that need attention at school the next day keep them from sleeping at night, and they cannot get the rest they need. It's a vicious cycle and one of the biggest reasons that educators are facing a systemic crisis of burnout, depletion, and compassion fatigue.

But it's not just educators who face societal pressures to blast through moments of connection and presence in the interest of checking tasks off a to-do list. All of us who are parenting or in the workforce right now were raised in these schools, and we were indoctrinated to celebrate anxiety and overwork. Those of us in codependent relationships, the helping professions, or who are people-pleasers are most likely in a similar quest for time to rest and recharge, and a never-ending race against the clock. After all, we have bills to pay, or we may get evicted and a schedule to keep, or we may lose our jobs.

Again, our corporatized society functions best when we are kept unaware that we have the innate ability to prioritize what really matters by reclaiming our attention, or that we have within us the power to create time and space for our own wellbeing. Keeping us on the hamster wheel keeps the money flowing into the hands of powerholders who least value our health and do not want us to choose how we use our time, because it would cut into their profits and strip them of their ability to control us.

We are misled to believe that the right thing to do is tend to others before ourselves, as a matter of worthiness and professional or personal duty. But just like on a depressurized airplane, we must put own oxygen masks on first, before we help those around us.

During week seven of an MBSR class, once they have extensively practiced building body awareness and working with difficult thoughts and feelings, participants are guided in the following exercise that helps them understand how their distribution of time for various activities impacts their stress levels.

Exercise 11.1: Balancing Nourishing and Depleting

With a blank piece of paper, make a list of everything you do in a normal day, from the moment you wake up until the moment you go to sleep.

Once your list is complete, label each item with an **N for nourishing**, or a **D for depleting**. Some items may go one way or another, depending on the day, so if you can't decide, you can label those **N/D**.

Examine the number of N's and the number of D's that you have and consider what kind of **balance** there is in your day. For the items that could be either N or D, consider what makes these items more nourishing or depleting on a given day? What conditions might support them becoming N's more often?

Identify which of your N's are the most nourishing for you, and label them **NN, making these items your non-negotiables**. How might you build the most nourishing items into your day so that you make sure they come first, thus prioritizing nourishment and wellbeing for yourself?

Reflection: Take a closer look at the first few items on your list, as the first few things you do in a day represent your highest priorities. How might you re-organize your tasks to support more nourishment and prioritization of wellbeing at the start of your day? What depleting items can you eliminate or move to later in the day?

This exercise can be a game-changer in the landscape of stress reduction. By identifying which activities are depleting, you can now set boundaries around those by allocating a fixed amount of time that you are **willing** to be **available** for these activities. Additionally, by clearly identifying your non-negotiables for self-care you can now set boundaries around these activities and **carve out time for them as an investment in your future self.**

I've led and participated in this activity dozens of times, and each time I do it I have more N's than the time before. Over time, I've learned to commit fiercely to my non-negotiables and have recognized that I can eliminate depleting activities (such as scrolling social media, watching violent shows on TV, or engaging in toxic communications with my ex) by setting boundaries for myself.

I've also noticed that the difference between an N/D activity being nourishing or depleting often comes down to how much time and energy I have, and whether I feel as if I am in choice about how I allocate my time, which influences the attitude and energy with which I engage in that activity.

Skill: Reclaim your Availability

You have the right to decide what you are available for and what you are not available for. Sometimes mapping this out explicitly gives you the opportunity to communicate this compassionately to those who are violating your boundaries without recognizing that they are doing so. You can enforce boundaries both by modeling what you are available for, and not participating in what you aren't available for. In a journal or blank sheet of paper, create a T-chart following the format of the one below.

I *Am* Available For...	I Am *Not* Available For...
-Calm, respectful communication at a scheduled time. -Responding to work emails between 9 am and 5 pm. -Caring conversations with a colleague or parent regarding a professional or personal concern -Cooking a meal and cleaning up after myself. -To share my practices and skills and clarify why I am dedicated to prioritizing my own wellbeing.	-Receiving angry text messages in the middle of the night. -Urgent emails that need a response late at night or first thing in the morning. -Being yelled at on the phone by a colleague or accosted in my office by an angry parent. -Dealing with a mess someone else left behind before cooking food for myself. -To justify how I allocate my time or explain myself to those who are not willing to understand.

You can use this language of availability to communicate your boundaries to others, without having to justify why you are saying no. For example, if my ex asks me to drop our daughter off at six p.m., and I've set her up with a playdate at a friend's house because I have a massage scheduled, I don't have to go into detail about why I can't drop her off or rub it in his face that I'm getting a massage, which would trigger a whole big thing. I can simply say, "I'm *not available* at that time. I *am available* to bring her to you at seven, or you are welcome to go and pick her up yourself at six."

In a professional environment, committing fiercely to your non-negotiables is a matter of survival. The language of availability is especially important for work-life balance because often you'll be asked to compromise your boundaries if you show even the slightest give. If you respond late at night to emails sent after five p.m., you are sending the message that you are available to work at all hours of the day. However, if you clearly communicate that you are not available to respond to email after five p.m., perhaps with an autoresponder or simply by modeling the boundary and resisting the temptation to do so, people will quickly learn not to expect a response from you until the morning. This is completely acceptable. In fact, it might even earn you respect and inspire others to set similar boundaries in their own lives.

Tips for Prioritizing Self-Care

1. Start your day with nourishing your own wellbeing.

Jon Kabat-Zinn calls this "tuning your instrument." Imagine that going into your day is like preparing to play a Mozart concerto. Take the time to tune your instrument (your mind) before playing the first notes. This might mean taking a few extra moments to quickly do a body scan before getting out of bed, listening to a guided mindfulness meditation, taking some time to stretch, and letting your body wake up, bringing awareness to your senses as you shower and brush your teeth, or simply resisting the temptation to check your phone or email first thing in the morning.

For me, this looks like setting my alarm a few minutes early, bringing my full attention to the process of making my coffee (savoring the smells, feeling my body as I wait for the water to boil, listening to the sounds of the liquid splashing into my favorite mug, and giving myself permission to savor the first few sips). People in my household also know that I stay in silence until after I have had my first cup of coffee and taken a few minutes to sit with it on my cushion and do at least 10 minutes of mindful breathing.

Starting the day with a few gentle moments of turning inward and tending to yourself will tone your nervous system for what is to come. Better yet, bookend your days. If you can give yourself time to practice for 10 or 15 minutes in the morning and evening, this will place a container of care around your entire day.

2. Every transition is an opportunity for a pause and a moment of somatic awareness.

Every time you shift from one activity to another is an opportunity to reset your attention. Each time you walk into your office, STOP, and take an intentional breath. Every time the phone rings, pause briefly, feel sensations in your body, then answer it. As you stand up from your chair, stretch your hands towards the ceiling or roll your shoulders.

Whenever you go through a doorway, take just a few seconds to feel the sensations of gravity in your body and the pressure of your feet connecting with the floor underneath you. Give yourself permission to come back to center as you move from one task or interaction to another. Access the five senses, feel the sensations of breath, move with awareness, or notice gravity. The more you practice this in moments of calm, the more available this skill will be to you in moments of crisis or overwhelm.

3. Create a container and ask for support in protecting your practice time.

It is not weakness to ask for help where you need it. Delegate the logistics of carving out time to a co-worker or administrative assistant if you have one. Let them know that you need five minutes to prepare and unwind before and after meetings and build this into your schedule. Make time for your own wellbeing before you commit to anything else.

If there is something in your schedule that happens regularly at a certain time of day, build a practice period into this event, before or after. Use this time to pause, take a few mindful breaths, just sit in silence, or do some gentle intentional movement. Use a "do not disturb" door hanger to protect your practice time, and educate staff, coworkers, and students to respect this, unless there is a true emergency that requires your immediate attention.

4. Find a buddy or invite others to practice mindfulness with you.

You can also build some accountability into your practice schedule by inviting an office colleague or friend to practice with you. Or you might sign up for the same online course or meditation app and check in with each other and review what practices you've done, share your reflections, and name any challenges you are facing in finding time to practice. A handful of online communities, such as Insight Timer can track your practice, connect you with others, and many skilled teachers offer guidance there.

5. Set fierce boundaries around technology (this is a big one).

- **<u>Use the "Do Not Disturb" feature</u>**: Download guided mindfulness practices that most support you to your phone or tablet ahead of time, so that you can be on airplane mode or at least do not disturb mode while you are listening. Most phones have this feature, and it will even let others know that you have notifications silenced and give them the option to "notify anyway." When I see this on people's messages, I do not automatically assume they are lazy or avoiding me. Rather, I feel a sense of genuine respect and appreciation that they are clearly setting boundaries around their availability to communicate at the moment.

- **Practice *not* checking your phone during certain periods of the day**: Avoid scrolling as a way of filling in-between/down time and resist the urge to look at your phone when you are in a meeting, waiting in line, sitting in traffic, or while you are resting. Not only does this protect you from being inundated with negative and toxic messaging, but it also sends a message to your nervous system that slowing down, tuning in (rather than tuning out), and just *being* is okay too.

- **Manage your notifications**: Turn off everything non-essential, so that you are not getting pinged and dinged every time someone likes an Instagram photo, or a cryptocurrency goes down in value. If there are people in your life whose communication rattles you or distracts you while you are at work, "hide alerts" on those messages.

- **Declutter your inbox (to the extent that you are able)**: Unsubscribe from everything extraneous that you can so that your email inbox is not filled with clutter and junk mail that can easily overwhelm you. Mark emails as *unread* if they need a response, otherwise swipe or click on them to "mark as read" to let yourself know that they do not need further attention. Your number of new messages in your inbox impacts your sense of overwhelm and should only reflect what immediately needs your attention. If the little red notification on your phone is regularly showing a number of emails in the thousands, this creates a ton of subliminal extra noise in your system around to-do items. Better yet, go into your settings and turn that little red flag off! You don't need to be reminded of how many messages you have every time you glance at your phone.

- **<u>Schedule digital communication</u>:** Set specific times when you will check and respond to emails and messages, put it on your calendar, and explicitly inform coworkers and friends of this so that they can manage their expectations around how long it might take you to respond. Have a separate notification system for emergencies and urgent communications or ask others to mark emails as urgent if they need an immediate reply.

Investing in My Future Self

I am a few years older and wiser now than I was when I experienced my first crippling back spasm at the age of 20. I've learned some things since then. First, there is nothing that robs you of your time quite like a debilitating injury that fills your moments with blinding pain and leaves you incapable of doing the things you love most. Second, if you do not tend to your wellness, you will be forced to tend to your illness. Third, I am where time comes from, and by fiercely committing to my non-negotiable nourishing practices each day, I stay in the driver's seat of my own life and have agency over my future wellbeing.

I have also learned not to blame my body for betraying me, and instead to respond with care to the pain by asking myself, *what does this have to teach me?* By slowing down enough to listen to the wisdom of my body, I have learned that a flicker of back pain is a signal to slow down and rest. It means that I am carrying too much, both literally and metaphorically, and I need to pause and bring some inquiry to how I am caring for myself. The foreboding tingle of numbness in my leg and the throb in my sciatic nerve are warning signs that my current pace and load are unsustainable, and that my body needs time and attention, or else it will break.

Over the years, and with each body scan, morning meditation, and mindful pause, I have gotten better at identifying the early warning signs that my burden is too heavy. Slowly, but surely, I am developing practices and skills to intervene on my own behalf *before* I am crumpled and spasming on the floor.

Each day when I wake up early before the sun, set a timer, and sit on my cushion, I reclaim my right to carve out time for my own wellbeing. Every time I choose to make myself a green smoothie filled with nutrients over a sugary snack, I invest in a future with less inflammation and more energy. By committing to sobriety from alcohol and drugs and being very intentional about what I bring in to my physical body and my awareness, I send my nervous system the message that I don't need to numb and go away from myself to be okay.

After all, what goes around comes around, and I've only got so many years to live and I'm not as young as I used to be. **The only time I truly have to invest in my future self is now.** If I wait, it could be too late. If I overdo it today by carrying too much, I am sure to feel it tomorrow. If I over-commit or put myself in a position where I am too pressured to perform or care for someone else, then I have doomed myself to the wracking anxiety that keeps me from sleeping at night and then the exhaustion spills over to those around me.

All of us are worthy of investing in our future selves and making the time to reprioritize our lives so that we can tend to what matters most first. When you feel as if time has been taken from you, pause, breathe, and remember that you are where time comes from. Reclaim it and take back your life.

Chapter 12: Reclaim Kindness

People pleasers have good intentions when they take on the burden of trying to make someone feel better. We truly just want to help and to offer our own wellbeing and happiness as a resource. After all, wouldn't the world be a better place if we could keep people from getting depressed? Not only is this endless output exhausting for the one doing all the work, but it also limits the other person from developing the skills to cultivate their own emotional health. Happiness takes effort and action, and if we believe it is our job to make the other person happy, and we take too much responsibility for their wellbeing, we may actually be leaving them in worse shape.

All I ever wanted was to make my ex-husband feel better. And at one point in the early days of our relationship, I was the only one who could. When he was down (which was often), I could cheer him up. When he was angry (also often), I could calm him down. When he thought life was pointless (again, often), I could inspire him and offer a glimmer of hope. Each time I was able to do this for him, I got a little dopamine hit, a little buzz of pleasure in my brain that told me I was valued, needed, and fulfilling my purpose.

What I didn't recognize at the time was that my enjoyment of the buzz would become an addiction, and that both of us would get hooked into a cycle of enabling and depression that could not end until the helping stopped. He couldn't heal until I stopped trying to heal for him. The act of kindness in this situation was to stop participating in the cycle.

The Trap of Enabling

My father is an altruist and enabler, so I learned from his example. From a young age my desire to be of service and to help those who could not help themselves was celebrated and encouraged. Being a helper, a caregiver, and a peacemaker was valued and needed in my chaotic home, which was filled with traumatized adopted children. Furthermore, I learned to get acknowledgment by being the one who didn't need help, cheered others up, and brought nourishment and resilience into the darkest places. Being a good person meant being a light in the darkness, even when I was low on energy.

Don't get me wrong, it is a wonderful thing to serve meals at the homeless shelter, to do service work in homes where people cannot afford upkeep and repairs, and to share the goodness of my heart with those who are suffering. However, it can easily go too far into the territory of over-helping and keeping people stuck in their own mess, especially when you have core beliefs that to be a "good person" and worthy of love you have to pour yourself out for others. We all need a little help from time to time, and sometimes it can be very challenging to ask for it. But the fine line between service and enabling is drawn when we overstep and offer help that compromises our own wellbeing, isn't asked for, and does not actually support recovery and repair.

Here's an example: My mom has always enjoyed tequila. She is not an over-drinker, but a casual sipper from time to time, and she is quite petite, so a little goes a long way. For as long as I can remember, she has kept a liquor cabinet and occasionally enjoyed a "special treat." My father, being the enabler that he is, purchases the tequila as he always has. One day, shortly after my mom left their assisted living apartment to join her friends for bingo, he heard a knock at the door. When he opened the door, there were two unfamiliar women and my drunk mother in a wheelchair, slurring and nearly unconscious.

"How did she get drunk?" my father asked.

The women did not know, and my drunk mother didn't know either. But when he went to the cabinet and checked the bottle of tequila he had just recently bought, he suddenly understood. Over the past few years, she has started to experience cognitive decline, and has been forgetting familiar faces and losing track of what day of the week it is. Both of my parents are in understandable denial, but the dementia is real, and it is progressing. My mom was drinking much more than she intended because it was a deeply engrained habit, and she simply didn't remember that she had already had a drink. As soon as he told me about this situation, he said, "I'm a life-long enabler. I don't know if I can stop."

"First of all, Dad, that's a belief you have about yourself but it's not necessarily true. You have to stop," I said. "It's not helping, it's hurting her. She doesn't need to have tequila available in the apartment. Just because you've always bought it for her doesn't mean you have to keep buying it. And you need to tell the staff about her cognitive decline so that they don't serve her too much at the bar."

Fortunately, he was able to see that I was right. But then he still had to face the hard part, answering to my confused mom who kept going to the cabinet for tequila, and demanding to know why it wasn't there. It didn't matter how many times my dad explained it to her. The dementia made it difficult for her to remember and put into context why something so familiar had changed. He had to deal with her frustration, again and again. In the face of that frustration, it may seem easier to throw your hands in the air and say, "fine. I'll get another bottle of tequila." But the act of kindness in this case is to draw the line and commit to it fiercely, even when it makes the other person unhappy or angry.

This situation with my parents is just one small example in which we can see the harm done by perpetuating a maladaptive habit cycle. Bringing awareness to the cycle is the first step to changing the pattern. Seeing the harm and reckoning with your own participation makes it easier to break free from the tendency to enable. In my own experience with depression and emotional abuse, this acknowledgment of my enabling and participation in the ongoing harm has been difficult to look at. All I have ever wanted was to help, and I never wanted to see how my efforts to help were hurting.

When you love someone, you want to help them feel better. But truthfully, there is only so much you can do for them. They have to want to be helped for anything you do to make a difference. It becomes enabling when you're either over helping someone who won't help themselves, or when you make it easy for them to stay stuck where they are. With my ex, who lashed out at me when he was triggered via digital communication, the act of kindness was to stop responding and eventually to block his text messages and filter his emails. When I finally mustered the strength to do this, it set both of us free. Without me responding to him, there was no continuation of the dialogue. Refusing to get hooked into the dynamic was like ignoring a playground bully, who gets no reward out of picking on you if you can shrug it off and not let it get to you.

Skill: How to Stop Enabling

Bring awareness to the enabling. Notice that what you are doing to help may be hurting. Ask yourself: Is my participation helpful? Are my efforts to help being received with appreciation? Did they ask me to help? Do they have the capacity to help themselves? Am I trying to do for them something only they can do for themselves?

Feel your feelings when you recognize that your help has actually caused harm. It's okay if you feel angry at yourself, sad, lost, irritated, exhausted. These feelings make sense given that you probably have expended a lot of effort that hasn't done much good in the end and has maybe even added to the other person's suffering. Become aware of sensations in your body that arise as you allow yourself to feel what you feel.

Set a boundary for yourself and others. Make this something clear and non-negotiable that you can commit to in the interest of stopping the cycle of enabling. In the case of emotional abuse, DO NOT ENGAGE. In the case of an addict, don't provide access to the drug. In the case of depression, don't offer to do something that the depressed person needs to do for themselves. You can join them or set them up for an activity (such as a hike or trip to a therapist), but you can't do the work for them.

Offer *yourself* the care that you want so much to offer to others. How can you turn your longing to be of service and to bring happiness to others toward yourself?

Forgive yourself and the other person. You cannot fight fire with fire. Holding onto bitterness and resentment not only hurts you, but it also perpetuates conflict. As an exercise, write a letter of forgiveness to yourself and the person you've been enabling.

Sometimes people need tough love. They need us to stop coddling them and draining ourselves of happiness in the hopes that they will absorb it. They may need professional support, fresh air, exercise, new skills for navigating difficulty, none of which you can do for them. You can drive them to therapy, but you can't heal for them. You can walk them outside into the sunshine, but you can't enjoy the warmth on their skin for them.

It took years for me to realize that it wasn't my job to make my ex-husband better, and even more years for me to learn that continuing to communicate with him about his mental health simply perpetuated the cycle. It was a hard lesson for me, and with it came big waves of grief. All I ever wanted was to help him be happy. And I failed. Maybe I even made it worse by trying.

As you can probably tell, I'm still working on the forgiveness piece. And that's okay, because I did the best I could with the tools I had available at the time. Now I know that not participating and disengaging is the act of kindness, even when every bone in my body wants to angrily pound out a bitter response and jab my finger at the send icon.

Loving Kindness for Others

We have already practiced sending kind thoughts to ourselves. The following is an extension of the loving kindness practice that offers us the opportunity to send kindness and care to those who need it the most.

The world is a troubled place full of heartache and pain, and I do my best to model to my daughter the agency it gives me when I send kindness towards people who are stressed, angry, bitter, and mean. It's not an easy shift, but it sure does feel better in my heart than letting their hatred and anger permeate me and define my actions.

One of the first ways I began practicing loving kindness for a difficult person was when I was behind the wheel and experienced the road rage, stress, or unsafe driving of another driver. Rather than getting myself worked up and angry about their unsafe driving, I tried to take a moment to consider the conditions that led to that person driving in such a careless way. Having been a stressed and suffering driver myself a few times, I know that unsafe driving often involves either tremendous anxiety and time pressure, *or* a total disregard for personal safety that comes from depression or very low self-worth. Either way, the person behind the wheel who is driving recklessly is likely to be suffering in some way.

Now, when someone zooms past me going too fast or driving aggressively, rather than getting angry and filling my car up with negative energy and difficult emotions, I choose to send them kind thoughts. I figure, if that person is happier, safer, healthier, calmer, then they won't have a need to drive in such a way that puts others in danger. There is nothing to be lost by sending kind thoughts in this situation, only my own peace of mind and regulation to be gained.

A similar approach benefits my rumination, interactions, and conflicts with my ex. When he lashes out at me with hostility, it does little good for me to retaliate or to stew and simmer in fury. Instead, if I can pause and ground myself, and recognize that his behavior is a symptom of his depression and a signal that he is struggling, then I can have compassion for him, without compromising my boundaries or needs. In fact, in many ways flipping the script in this way and sending kindness in response to aggression is a way of setting a fierce boundary, reclaiming my mental real estate, stepping in the driver's seat, choosing not to participate in the violence, and taking back my right to be peaceful.

We all deserve to be peaceful, and the more peaceful and happy others are, the less they will lash out and cause harm, right? The practice of sending kind thoughts to those who have made our lives difficult is where the rubber meets the road. It's not easy, but it's how we can start to shift the needle away from anger, blame, shame, and rage to understanding, compassion, care, and curiosity.

These phrases may be challenging at first, especially if you are angry or highly self-critical, have been a victim of sexual, emotional, or physical abuse, or your mind is simply not in the habit of thinking this way. Please feel free to go as slowly as you need to. Remember to resource yourself by staying in choice. Open your eyes if you need to. Shift your attention to one of the senses or your breath. Move your body, and orient to the present moment.

In our highly critical and judgmental world, this way of attending to ourselves and others with kindness can be a radical act, and it is important to start small, in ways that are manageable, so that you don't become overwhelmed. Before we jump into sending kind thoughts to a difficult person, which can be hard if we are unfamiliar with this practice, it can be helpful to begin by sending kind and loving thoughts to someone whom you already feel kindness towards, or a person or teacher who has been supportive in your life. You can practice loving-kindness in any posture, seated, standing, lying down, or even walking.

The full instructions are provided below, and the first time you do this exercise, you may find it supportive to access the 14-minute recording available at fierceboundaries.com.

<u>Exercise 12.1: Loving Kindness for Others</u>
(Including a Difficult Person)

Adopt a posture that feels comfortable and take a few grounding breaths to stabilize your attention, noticing the body sitting and becoming aware of the sensations of air moving into and out of the body. Bring your awareness to the area of your heart. You might even choose to place a hand on your heart, or to offer some other gesture to yourself of care and support.

When you are ready, bring to mind the image of a friend, family member, teacher, or mentor — someone, either alive or passed, who has been supportive to you. This might be someone who is a resource for you in troubled times, and a source of compassion and wisdom. This does not have to be someone you know intimately or at all and could even be a pet or a spiritual being. Hold this being in your loving awareness and silently repeat these wishes:

May you be happy.

May you be healthy.

May you be safe and protected.

May you be free from harm.

May you live with ease.

May you be free from enmity. May no hatred fill your heart.

And as you offer these kind wishes to this person, allow whatever emotions arise, and notice any physical sensations you experience. Take some time to rest here for a few moments, bathing in the kindness of the wishes you have sent to this beloved being.

Now, bring to mind the image of someone who may be the source of some difficulty in your life. This might be a difficult relationship, or a challenging dynamic with a colleague. If this is your first time doing this practice, it's important to choose someone who feels manageable (not the *most* difficult person).

Allow the image of this person to take shape in front of you, checking in with the felt experience in the area of your heart. Take a moment to get a sense for their physical features, the way that they carry themselves in the world, a sense of their story, and all the pieces of their life that have made them a source of difficulty for you. You might even imagine adversity or challenges that this person may have faced, or some quality of love or kindness that they may not have had the opportunity to experience. And once this person is clearly present in your awareness, as best you can, offer the following wishes.

May you be happy.

May you be healthy.

May you be safe and protected.

May you be free from harm.

May you live with ease.

May you be free from enmity. May no hatred fill your heart.

May you receive love, in all its forms.

Repeat each of these wishes as many times as you would like. When you are ready, gently allow the image of this difficult person to recede and bring your attention back to the area of the heart. At this point, you might choose to place a hand on your heart and feel the sensations of contact here. Take a few heart-centered breaths and acknowledge any emotions that arise by naming and allowing them to be here.

Now, expand the awareness to include a sense of all beings, including yourself at the center. Allow yourself to include animals, plants, dictators, populations of entire countries, even microscopic organisms, and all the people spread across the earth, alive and passed, all of us connected through gravity, the rhythm of the seasons, the rising and setting of the sun and moon, our heartbeats, and the cycle of the breath. With this sense of all beings in your awareness, offer these wishes:

May all beings be happy.

May all beings be healthy.

May all beings be safe and protected.

May all beings be free from harm.

May all beings live with ease.

May all beings be free from enmity. May no hatred fill our hearts.

May all beings know kindness and compassion.

May all beings know love and receive it in all its forms.

Take a few moments to rest here, in this awareness of our shared experience of aliveness on this earth, and the breath that connects us all. Maybe you can even take a moment to thank your heart for its infinite capacity for love, tending to your heart, noticing any sensations or emotions that are present and welcoming them. Become aware of any physical sensations around the heart, remembering that in holding yourself with compassion, and in extending wishes of kindness to others, even those whom you may find challenging, that you are being a light in the darkness and expanding the love and connectedness between all human beings.

Reflection: What showed up for you in this practice? Spend a few minutes journaling and exploring any thoughts or feelings that arose as you sent kind wishes. For many people, this is a very new way of practicing, and it can feel awkward or uncomfortable to repeat these phrases. Even if it does not feel natural or fluid, energy follows thought and the very act of imagining kindness has an impact, sending ripples of care into the world and helping you build new neural pathways.

Fear Begets Fear, Love Begets Love

Sometimes, when I feel frightened, or find myself in a situation where I'm uncertain about my safety or the intentions of someone who feels threatening, I use these loving kindness phrases as a mantra to stabilize my nervous system.

Once, I was out walking on a remote trail late in the evening and it was getting dark. I saw two large men walking toward me along the path, and no one else was around. I felt a churning in my gut and my heart rate quickened as I noticed that both men were wearing face masks with skulls on them (this was before Covid, so these kinds of masks were not common, and it didn't seem cold enough to justify such a face covering).

Their appearance was threatening, and the closer they got, the more I sensed (or interpreted) violent intentions.

Because I practiced mindfulness meditation and had recently spent a lot of time repeating these loving kindness phrases during a retreat, they were available to me on the tip of my tongue. Noticing that my fear was growing, I shifted my attention to the area of my heart and started repeating to myself: *May you be happy. May you be peaceful. May you be safe and protected. May you be free from worry. May NO HATRED FILL YOUR HEARTS.* I did everything I could to radiate love and kindness through my heart space and to send these men feelings of unconditional positive regard.

When they drew close enough for me to hear their footsteps, one of the men veered from the path and started walking straight at me. As he reached a distance of about six feet away, I focused all of my attention on my heart, feeling it pounding in my chest, directed an energetic feeling of love towards him as I exhaled, smiled, and said, "enjoy your walk. It's a beautiful night."

He gave a subtle nod, shifted his trajectory, and walked past me. I continued to repeat the phrases to myself as I breathed in and out: *May you be happy. May you be peaceful. May you be safe. May you be free from harm.*

Once I sensed that the distance between us had increased to about fifty feet, I looked over my shoulder, saw that they were still walking away from me, and started to shake.

I have no idea what their true intentions were, but those men scared the daylights out of me. I do know that if I had shown my fear by cowering and shrinking away or trying to outrun them, it would have been much more likely for something awful to happen.

Fear begets fear and love begets love. When we are afraid of someone or something, as in the case of the young woman who shut down Denver schools that day, we react and clench and brace with tension and apprehension. This impacts our interactions with others, our stress levels, our release of adrenaline and cortisol, and our heart-mind coherence. If you've ever witnessed a dog or a hornet respond to someone who is afraid, you've probably seen this play out. They say dogs and hornets can smell fear and it triggers them to attack. When we are afraid, we are more likely to act carelessly and do things we regret. We are also more likely to trigger a fear/aggression reaction in someone else.

Hurt people hurt people, but healed people heal people. And the more love we put out into the world, the more those who have been hurt will have the capacity to love others. What you can do in the face of bullying and abuse is recognize that when people are outwardly mean, their internal dialogue towards themselves must be even worse. If my ex bullied me with such venom and fury, I couldn't imagine how much he bullied himself. So, rather than engage in communication with him, I did the only thing that I could, I tried to forgive myself and him, and sent him kind thoughts, wishes of healing, and compassion towards his wounded little boy who made up that he deserved to be treated so horribly.

If someone doesn't know how to show love to others, chances are it's because they didn't get to feel that love from their caregivers growing up. What they need now is not for us to be afraid of their anger, but to be seen and witnessed, and loved even though they are hurting. We don't have to over-involve ourselves in their lives to offer this love. In fact, our boundaries allow us to be love, to cultivate gardens of care and compassion, and to model the willingness to be human and to bear witness, without turning away.

The way we can love an imperfect world is to let kindness be our default, rather than defensiveness. We can meet pain and suffering by radiating love and goodness from our own hearts, rather than cowering and preparing for battle. We can turn poison into medicine and shine a light on the goodness in people, until they remember that they are lovable. This is how we heal a traumatized world.

"No act of kindness, no matter how small, is ever wasted."
-Aesop[20]

Chapter 13: Interrupt the Trauma Cycle

On a societal level, we as a people are traumatized. With 67% of the population scoring at least one ACE (Adverse Childhood Experience), the majority of us are walking around with generations of trauma stored in our bodies. Additionally, in family systems, this trauma is often un-addressed and re-enacted, and passed down through generations, creating a systemic pathology that involves widespread depression, anxiety, substance use disorders, dysregulation, and heightened states of arousal.

When someone has experienced a life-threatening event, natural disaster, witnessed an act of violence, or seen harm or injury enacted on others, their perceptions can become disoriented, or they may even dissociate and feel like they have left their body. When trauma is not metabolized or integrated, survivors may become "stuck" in a **trauma** response or state of fight, flight, or freeze. Their attention may be repeatedly and unpredictably hijacked into thoughts or images about the threatening event, or their body may be immobilized or agitated with undischarged traumatic energy.

For some trauma survivors, the triggers that alert them to danger or the act of scanning for threat can be constant. This can be experienced as hyper-vigilance, exaggerated startle response, sheer panic or terror, flashbacks to the traumatic event, intense shame, a feeling of not being able to navigate the world correctly, heightened sensitivity to benign stimuli, even an aversion or mistrust of every person of a certain size and shape or gender. When these circumstances occur in the absence of supportive human connection and safe relationships, the result is often maladaptive coping and the perpetuation of cycles of abuse.

Mass shootings, terrorism, relational violence, and systemic oppression are symptoms of systemic dysregulation and collective trauma that has compounded generation after generation. We are living in a traumatized world and the odds are stacked higher against us day by day.

Emotional Violence *is* Domestic Abuse

Voice notes, emails, and text messages don't leave purple marks that can be covered up with makeup or disguised with sunglasses. But a domestic partner's episodes of emotional violence can leave you trembling, hyper-vigilant, rattled, and afraid, just like a physical attack. The damage may be hidden, but the trauma is real. There may not be eyewitnesses, video footage that would stand up in court, or a single, identifiable incident of acute threat, but ongoing **psychological**

maltreatment is a legitimate cause of complex post-traumatic stress disorder that can leave deep scars.

When I entered into my relationship with my ex, I had no way of knowing that not enoughness was etched into my DNA – that I chose an emotionally abusive spouse because it felt like normal to my deeply wounded child and ancestral parts. Even though his words were just lines on the screen of my phone, they pounded me over and over again like kicks to the kidneys, leaving me bruised and bleeding internally. Other than the way my body buckled and strained under the emotional weight of the continuous abuse, there was never any external evidence of an attack.

He seemed to time his attacks strategically so that I never got to experience peace, with messages always arriving just when I was starting to rest and sink into the quiet of solitude, creative work, or recovery from the last battery of accusations.

But if he never hits you, does it still count as abuse? I found myself wondering this one afternoon as my heart hammered in my chest and my trembling thumbs pounded a response into my phone. I had been gnawing on my nails and fighting a panic attack since my ex picked our daughter up earlier that afternoon, and now he was texting me about how worthless his life was, while driving over Poncha Pass with her in the back seat.

Ding. "I want you to suffer," he wrote. The words battered me like fists as they bounced through my thoughts and twisted in my gut. I couldn't help but think that if he really wanted me to suffer, driving over a cliff and taking her with him would certainly do the trick. Could he stoop that low though? Hurt her to hurt me. God, I hoped not.

In between messages, I typed my question into google and got the following answer: **"Abuse means to intentionally or recklessly cause or attempt to cause bodily injury to you... or to molest, attack, hit, stalk, threaten, batter, *harass*, telephone, or *contact you...* or to *disturb your peace.* Abuse can be spoken, written, or physical."**

While various sites had different definitions, and most legal resources referred to domestic violence as a physical act of aggression, the National Domestic Violence Hotline site[21] gave me a list of red flags to help me determine whether what I was experiencing qualified as "emotional abuse."

I share the following information with you, not just so that you can bring awareness to emotional abuse in your own life, but also so that you can recognize the signs of psychological maltreatment of your loved ones. Below are just a few of the red flags to watch out for in relational dynamics.

Warning Signs of Emotional Abuse

- Your partner name calls you or demeans you.
- Intimidating you with threatening looks, actions, or gestures.
- Destroying your belongings or your home.
- Your partner tries to control you, your time, and your actions.
- Your partner shifts blame back to you to avoid responsibility or questions your reality. This is called **gaslighting**.
- Your partner is critical of your appearance.
- Your partner is jealous of time spent with your friends or family.
- Your partner makes threats to hurt you or others to get what they want.
- Your partner embarrasses you in public.
- Your partner does not trust you and acts possessive.
- Your partner threatens breaking up, abandonment, or divorce to manipulate an argument.
- Your partner threatens suicide during arguments.
- Your partner blames you for their unhealthy/abusive behaviors.

How to help: The best way to support a friend or family member who is on the receiving end of emotional abuse is to shower them with love and reminders of their worthiness. It is **not** advised to intervene on their behalf, stand up to the abuser, or call the police unless your loved one asks you to do so or if they are in imminent danger. Do not put yourself in harm's way or try to do for them what they need to do for themselves.

Instead, continually remind them of their beauty, strength, and capacity to set fierce boundaries. Help them get educated on trauma bonding, the chemical "addiction" to love, and strategies they can implement to disengage and stop participating in the abusive behavior. You might even find it helpful to buy them a copy of this book.

Use the word "survivor" instead of "victim." A victim mindset can keep people stuck and cause them to over-identify as an abused person rather than as someone who is worth protecting. This switch can support survivors to take agency, manage their impulses to engage in the abusive dynamic, become the conductor of their attention, and reclaim their right to peace, safety, and wellbeing.

As for my own story, I don't need to share with you the pages and pages of awful words that were exchanged, with subtext that was terrifying enough to send me into a spiral of panic and fear. I don't have to paint the scene for you so that you can know what it was like to discover my ex's name burned into the wall of the garage, or so that you can feel the visceral churning of the fire that boiled inside me when his test messages accused *me* of child abuse. I don't need to explain the thought process that led me to wonder whether I should change my phone number, learn how to use a gun, pick up some pepper spray, or keep a baseball bat next to the door.

If you find yourself wondering whether something is abuse or domestic violence, that alone is enough to seek help. You do not need a court or a mediator to tell you that what is happening to you is not OK. You do not need to compromise your values, or your sense of belonging in your body to make a relationship work.

Just like you might feel the need to justify your reasons for a divorce like I did, being unhappy, and feeling like you are hiding yourself, and cowering in fear of not belonging is reason enough. You are enough.

The bottom line is that a loving relationship should make you feel emotionally safe to be your authentic self, rather than exhausted and scared of doing or saying the wrong thing. Whether it's friendship love or romantic love, love should lift you up. Love should make you feel like the best version of yourself. You should come away from interactions with people who love you feeling full and energized, nourished, cared for, regarded, and respected. You should feel like the truest, most beautiful version of yourself when you're around people who claim to love you. Otherwise, it's not love, and you deserve better.

The first step to healing these wounds is to acknowledge that a trauma has occurred, and to recognize that you cannot do it alone. The symptoms of emotional abuse include feeling trapped, like the situation is your own fault, and believing that if you ask for help you are being a burden. Reaching out can take a lot of courage, but there are resources available to you. You deserve peace and safety, and you are not alone.

A mental health professional can help you to remove yourself from the unsafe situation and create space for you to give yourself permission to feel the grief and anger that you feel. If you do not have the financial resources for therapy, you can start by calling the National Domestic Violence Hotline at 1-800-799-SAFE or texting "START" to 88788.

Finally, it's important to remember that hurt people hurt people. Blaming and shaming your abuser for their behaviors does nothing to stop the cycle of abuse, it only perpetuates it and keeps you engaged in the never-ending battle. Abusive behaviors are rooted in childhood experiences of psychological maltreatment or neglect and come from a place of core wounding in relationship to belonging in the body and in the world.

Rather than blaming or vilifying your abuser, which does not help anyone heal, see if you can find a small amount of compassion or care for the wounded child inside them that learned from experience to treat people so poorly. **This does not mean allowing the abuse to continue.** Also, remember that when people are externally abusive and mean on the outside, often they are much more critical internally. As awful as their words and actions towards you might be, see if you can send some kindness to their inner self-critic. They are probably meaner to themselves than they are to anyone else, and all because they are desperately seeking the love they were taught they didn't deserve.

I know this is a hard pill to swallow, and if it's difficult or impossible to bring care and compassion to someone who has hurt you, this is completely understandable. Just remember, your practices of forgiveness, kindness, and compassion do not mean accepting abusive behaviors or allowing ongoing abuse. Rather, they are boundaries you can set and interventions you can take on your own behalf to shift your own relationship to the wounded parts of the abuser, to step out of fear-based thinking, reactivity, and fight/flight, and choose a response that is more regulating and stabilizing within your own nervous system.

How to Stop the Cycle

1. Learn to pause in moments of reactivity, anchor your awareness in the present moment, and *feel your feelings rather than think your feelings*. Give yourself some space to choose a response rather than react. If avoidance arises in your relationships, take some time to notice what you feel and give yourself permission to have the experience you are having. Remember that thoughts aren't facts and take the time to investigate what arises with curiosity, rather than being driven by deeply engrained patterns of fear or avoidance.

2. Honor the wisdom of fear and avoidance and respect your protective strategies. Running away from relationships may have been what kept you safe from being abandoned, exiled, betrayed, or neglected in the past. Avoidance and fear are the brain's intelligent responses to danger, and when your nervous system is signaling you that a relationship is unsafe, slow down, ground attention with your senses, and take the time to evaluate from a place of resource and present-moment somatic awareness.

Sometimes the strategies you developed when you were young and deciding how the world worked may no longer be relevant or useful in the present moment. See if you can step out of impulsive or habitual ways of relating to intimacy, slow down, turn inward, acknowledge that avoidance had an important, protective role, and listen to the wisdom of your body as it offers you real-time information about what's here, now.

Look for red flags and warning signs but know that this relationship is not necessarily the same as others that hurt you. There may be other options and different conditions than those that were unsafe in the past or created the feeling of not belonging when you were young.

3. Spend time with your wounded child parts. Welcome yourself to be your own person having a unique human experience. Gather and surround yourself with images of yourself as a young child, during the time when you learned to be avoidant or fearful. Notice what arises in your body as you connect with this younger, wounded part of yourself. Is there anything that your avoidant/scared parts want you to know? What needs weren't met? Or is there something that they want to say or hear? As you engage in this inquiry, what shows up in your felt experience?

4. Affirm your worthiness. Say it out loud. Believe you are worthy of safety, care, and attention, and reinforce this with your language. Surround yourself with affirmations and positive messaging, enough to counteract the persistent negative messaging coming from the media, generational trauma, and post-traumatic programming. Each moment of attending to yourself is a radical act of self-love that rewires your brain. Every time you give yourself the opportunity to turn your attention inward, you are sending yourself a message that you are worthy of care and attention. *You are enough. You deserve care and attention. You are worthy of safety and love.*

5. Give yourself regular opportunities for rhythmic sensory input. The more you include rhythm and sensory awareness in your day-to-day activities, the more you can widen the window of tolerance, and offer yourself the experience of predictability, regulation, and rhythm that strengthens heart coherence and gives your wounded little one the missing experience of safety and stability. Drumming, dancing, playing a musical instrument, walking, swaying, horseback riding, and rocking motions are all ways to soothe the parts of your nervous system that developed in an unpredictable and threatening environment.

6. Externalize grief, fear, and rage. Undischarged traumatic energy stored in muscle tissue can wreak havoc on your body and mind. When big, unintegrated emotions are trapped in our cellular memory, we can have trouble discerning perceived threats based on triggers from benign stimuli. Healing and integration occur when we can feel the feelings related to the trauma, while grounded in the safety of present moment experience. Intentional writing, movement, somatic therapy, creating art or music, and spending time in nature can support this somatic release of undischarged energy from the body.

Somatic Release

When we have no steam vent, and the source of our outrage comes from beyond our cognitive experience and understanding, it may eventually explode out of us, and can cause great harm. As I have explored working somatically with the rage energy in my own system, I have discovered several practices that support me in physically externalizing this energy without causing harm to myself or others.

Please keep in mind that underneath of rage is often buried grief and sadness, and that the process of externalizing these big emotions may reveal deeper layers of unresolved and unintegrated feelings. It can be supportive to engage in these practices with the guidance and care of a therapist or compassionate friend who is willing to make space for you to express the truth of your feelings without trying to fix them. It is possible to do these practices for and by yourself, just be aware that you may not be immediately prepared to return to work, parenting responsibilities, or relational interaction after making space to release these powerful and often overwhelming emotions.

So, when you choose to engage in these practices, my recommendation is to carve out enough time and space for yourself to recover and integrate the experience, at least for the rest of the day. Plan to spend that time tending to yourself with exquisite kindness. Avoid activities that take your awareness away from yourself or tax your body, such as drinking alcohol, drugging, bingeing, doom scrolling, multi-tasking, etc. Instead, see if you can allow the entire day to be a day of reflection and present-moment awareness, dedication to your own wellbeing, and if possible, a return to the natural world and to honoring yourself. You might choose to journal, paint, dance, hike, play music, workout, meditate, cook a nourishing meal, write a letter to your child or future self, or engage in any other activity that supports nourishing your own wellbeing.

Exercise 13.2: Practices for Somatic Release

Nature-Based Practices:

- Collect heavy rocks that represent the burdens you are carrying and gather them in one place with some care. One at a time, thank your burdens for what they have helped you learn, then release them by throwing them into a river, or off a cliff and scream or cry.

- Use sticks, rocks, and other nature materials to build something that represents the object of your anger, use your words or your voice to express your feelings towards the object, thank the object for what it has taught you, and then smash what you built.

- Make a clearing and ask the trees and nature beings to bear witness to you as you dance your story, letting your feelings and experience move through your body. Be aware of your body's limits, take care not to injure yourself, and keep yourself grounded by staying in contact with gravity and sensations.

- Drum your feelings and/or your heartbeat. You can do this with nature objects, such as sticks against a tree trunk, with your hands on your heart, or with a handheld drum, if you have one. Move your body rhythmically as you emote. Remember to breathe.

- Using materials gathered from nature, create a piece of art that represents what you are ready to leave behind. When you feel ready, thank yourself for this creative process, then walk away from your creation without looking back. If it feels appropriate, you might choose to create a second art piece, a circle of stones or branches that you can step into or collect an object from nature that represents what you are moving towards.

- Lay down on the earth and allow yourself to dissolve or melt into the ground. Bring awareness to the fact that the earth is holding you, and everything you are carrying. Feel the sensations of your breathing and gravity in your body. You might even choose to dig a small hole with your hands or a stick and lie face down with your face in the hole. Speak, cry, or scream into the earth, expressing whatever you no longer wish to carry. When you have finished, use your hands to push the dirt back into the hole, giving your burdens to the earth.

- Interact with the trees. Tell them the story of your wounding, and ask them to tell you their story. Spend time listening to them, playing with them, taking on their shapes with your body, and connecting with their histories. Whether it is just picking up a pinecone, snapping off a branch, or a pulling apart a leaf, or another way that you can bring your 5 senses to a part of the tree, they are available to remind you of your rootedness and connectedness to the earth. You can lean your back against the trunk of a tree or sink your hands into the soil around the roots, climb into the tree, or bury your nose in the bark. Trees are an ever-available invitation to return to the present moment and re-awaken the mind in the here and now.

- Start a rooftop garden, volunteer at a community garden, ride your bike to a farm stand, or find creative ways to engage your senses and move your body in service of gathering, preparing, and eating fresh produce.

For some of you, finding places in nature where you can be in solitude and tend to your feelings without concern for the perceptions or needs of others may not be possible, but with some creativity you can modify these practices to suit your living situation and to keep yourself and others safe. Some other healthy, safe ways to transform/externalize rage energy when you live in a city or close to others are included below.

Indoor Somatic Release Practices:

- Put your feet, or your whole body, in cold water to tone your Vagus Nerve. If you do not have access to clean water outdoors, you can run cold water in the bath over your feet or turn the shower water to cold for a few minutes. When you do this, notice the sensations without bracing, tensing, or trying to pull away as best you can. Allow yourself to get curious about what you are feeling physically. See if you can relax your muscles, investigate how the sensations let you know you are alive, and welcome any discomfort as an opportunity to strengthen and stabilize attention with something that is happening right now, in the present moment, in your own control.
- Scream or sing in your car, as loud as you need to. Or scream into a pillow, underwater in a swimming pool or bath, or with your hands over your mouth.
- Push against a wall with all your strength and make a sound that goes with this motion (one that comes from deep in your gut). You might even imagine you are pushing away an attacker or pushing off the weight of the world. If you have a willing and resourced friend, you can also do this exercise by pushing hands. Before you begin, take some grounding breaths together and make agreements about safety, such as a time-out word and how strongly you want your friend to resist. This activity may evoke big feelings, and that's okay. As best you can, allow them to move out of your body.
- Chant, howl at the moon, participate in group singing, or play your feelings on an instrument of your choice.
- 5Rhythms, Ecstatic Dance, martial arts, Qi Gong, yoga, or any other sober rhythmic movement activity.
- Kundalini breathing or other breathwork exercises that also involve

rhythmically moving the body.

- Individual or group exercise or movement activity that gets you sweating. Imagine that the sweat is your emotional and physical toxicity leaving your body.

- Write an anger letter, or a letter from your rage (what does rage want to say or do?), read it out loud, then rip it into pieces, burn, or destroy it. Then go for a walk or run or shake your body to discharge energy.

- Brush discharged energy off your body with a sweeping motion towards the floor. Place your hands on the ground to give to the earth what is no longer useful for you to hold.

- Plant a small indoor herb garden from seeds, even if it is just a single potted plant. Put the soil into the pot with your bare hands and take the time to feel the sensations of earth against your skin. Choose herbs that are aromatic, have medicinal properties, or are useful in cooking. With each seed you push into the soil, set an intention that supports nourishing your own wellbeing. Place it in a location by a window that receives some sunlight, and water it regularly. Take time each day to appreciate how tending to the seeds you planted supports the growth of your positive intentions.

Chapter 14: A Light in the Darkness

When people used to make fun of me in middle school, my father would tell me, "You're too sensitive. Don't let them get to you." But I had no idea *how* to do this because I was, by nature, a highly sensitive person, and I felt *everything*. I had no way to distinguish my own experience from others, I was permeable like a sponge, and words and glares and judgment of my peers shot right through me, lingering for hours or days while I ruminated on how I could do better, and be what I thought the world wanted me to be. I bit my nails and picked my scabs, always trying to smooth myself out by ripping pieces of myself away.

I had little self-respect and fewer boundaries, and I pushed myself to the edge of sanity trying to be good enough. When I was growing up, I never understood that I was worthy of giving myself the respect and dignity that I longed for in relationships, and I never learned how to effectively stand up for myself, and to honor my individuality and right to physical and emotional safety.

I was desperate to belong and desperate to be like my peers, so that I could fit somewhere with my lumpy arms and my freckled skin. I didn't value my body, and I gave myself away too many times, first to sexual encounters with men who berated me, then to drugs and alcohol, then to a marriage with a person who drained the joy out of every room and continued to belittle and harass me for years after our divorce. I was an empath, full of holes from feeling so much of the world's pain and trying to make everything better by compromising myself, holes where anyone could easily slip in and steal my light, take advantage of how much I cared, and take a piece of my heart with them.

My father's advice was good, but I didn't know *how* to be less sensitive. I cared and felt too much not to let them get to me. The message that my nervous system received was that my sensitivity was a problem, that big feelings were to be contained behind closed bedroom doors, and that I was "ready to come back out and be part of the family again" once I had packed my emotions away so they wouldn't spill over onto anyone else.

The hurt and desperation built up inside me, and I contained myself because I thought that was what I had to do to take care of everyone else. But like a churning volcano without a steam vent, I would eventually explode. My rage and fury would pour out of me in a torrent, and I would get red-faced and scream and smash things and shout bitter and violent words that I would later regret. This explosive behavior continued through the divorce and on a few occasions (I'm so sorry to say) even terrified my daughter. I certainly didn't want to be a raging mother with unpredictable behavior that would surely fill her with her own explosive anger and land her in therapy.

The years since my divorce have been filled with opportunities for post-traumatic growth and to practice setting boundaries and reclaiming all the pieces of myself that I gave away. When I found my biological family, at the age of 42, on Ancestry.com, I learned about the legacy of alcoholism and abuse that led to my birthmother being in such an unstable domestic violence situation that she had no choice but to put me up for adoption. I saw pictures of my biological father drunk and high and found the police records from when he stole firearms and assaulted women. I learned that I came from a family characterized by rejection, addiction, and rage, and I became determined to do it differently for my daughter.

Once I learned these truths about my heritage, my body could no longer tolerate alcohol, drugs, or the presence of men, and for a time I developed a somatic allergic reaction to any substances that put strain on my liver. The writing was on the wall. I had no choice but to make real changes and get control of myself. What I quickly realized with the clarity of sobriety was that I had been letting the world fill me with many forms of toxic waste, and that I could make different choices about what I gave away and what I allowed to permeate me. What if I regarded my physical, mental, emotional, and spiritual body with exquisite care? What if I treated myself like a temple? What if I held my wounded heart with the tenderness of a newborn baby and welcomed myself to belong in my body again?

Just like in addiction/recovery work, there are moments of relapse and ongoing repair. But each time I summon the strength to set or reset a fierce boundary, honor my humanness, feel my feelings, and respect the wisdom of my body, it is an opportunity to reparent myself, and to reconnect across time and space with the wounded little one inside me who felt so much of other people's pain. Sometimes these moments of mothering myself look like staying in the car when I pick my daughter up from her dad's instead of going inside his house. Sometimes it's simply shifting my attention away from one of his death glares, sitting on the other side of the room during recitals and school performances, or saying "no" to another request for money. Each time I enforce a boundary out of love for my wounded parts and for my daughter's right to have a regulated mother, there is a little girl inside me who gets a little stronger in her sense of belonging in her body and feels a little bit more deserving of love.

Takeaway Skills for Self-Healing

"Know Thyself" — Take intentional time to get familiar with your own experience, including the tone of your self-talk, your go-to coping mechanisms, your attachment style, your protective strategies, and your relational habits. Reconnect with your wounded parts and learn to identify your triggers. Slow down when you notice discomfort, and ask yourself, *what's here?*

Cultivate Physical Literacy — learn to listen to subtle signals from your nervous system, notice how you hold your body in different situations, and bring awareness to areas of the body that are chronically tensing or bracing for an attack. Regularly reconnect to your felt experience through sensory awareness practices, trauma-informed yoga, body scan meditation, massage, dance/movement meditation, exercise, and mindful walking.

Cultivate Emotional Literacy — Build awareness of what you notice in your body as you observe and bring curiosity to an emotion. ***Feel your feelings, rather than think your feelings.*** Allowing yourself to feel what you feel is a way of welcoming yourself to have your own experience. Ask yourself, *how can I best take care of myself, given what is* *arising?* Practice the Soften, Soothe, Allow Meditation or Loving Kindness.

Cultivate Mental Literacy – Remember that thoughts aren't facts. Get to know how your mind works through journaling, awareness of thoughts meditation, and periods of internal reflection and silent sitting. Spend a few minutes each day being with yourself, giving yourself space to be just as you are, and when you notice judgment or self-critical thoughts arise, pause and replace them with compassionate messages of care and unconditional positive regard.

Honor your Non-negotiables – Enforce your non-negotiables by building time for them into your schedule and consistently sticking with it. Get clear about what you are available for and what you are not available for. Make a T-Chart, or written commitment to yourself, and post it somewhere visible as a reminder. Communicate these boundaries and set expectations for yourself and others so that they respect your non-negotiables as much as you do.

Honor your Body's Wisdom and Take Your Time – Establish safe anchors for attention first, before diving into the deep end. Honor the wisdom of barriers and protective strategies and avoid retraumatizing yourself by over-attending to traumatic stimuli. Use the skills of resourcing, pendulation, and orienting with the senses to stay grounded in your present moment experience.

Say it Out Loud – The words you use matter. Be aware of the language you use to talk about emotions ("anger is present" or "I feel angry" rather than "I *am* angry"). Put a stop to self-critical thoughts and judgments. Post affirmations where you frequently see them, and practice saying phrases like "I am enough" until you believe them.

When you hear someone else speaking poorly of themselves, stop them and say, "please don't talk about my friend that way."

Take Agency – Make decisions informed by your own knowing and take action to get your needs met on a regular basis. Speak up for yourself and don't allow yourself to be trapped into neglecting your wellbeing by the perceived expectations of others. Even small actions and investments in your health, such as standing to stretch during a meeting, can engage the pre-frontal cortex and keep you from spiraling into depression or anxiety.

Move Your Body and Take Up Space – You don't have to shrink yourself to fit into someone else's life. Stretch your limbs, move your body frequently and to your own rhythm, and do not let the world confine you into a prison of not belonging. *It is your birthright to belong in your body, and no one can take that away from you.*

Post Traumatic Growth

The reality of the world we live in is that so many of us must keep going even amid ongoing grief, fear, relational drama, trauma triggers, and perpetual threat. And so many of us are doing so caught in a habit loop that was often cemented by our ancestors. When we ask, *what is this trying to teach me?* we have an opportunity to shed some light on our deeply patterned ways of doing things that are no longer serving us. These are strategies that we learned (often by watching and responding to our caregivers) during our earliest years to belong and to keep ourselves safe. At the time they were the best we could do with the information we had available. They were wise and protective strategies for getting our needs met, and essential for our survival. However, when we carry these strategies into our adulthood and continue to replay them in our relationships, they can keep us stuck in the same quagmire as our parents, and their parents, and all the generations of alcoholic, abused, and oppressed men and women going back and back and back.

They say the cracks are where the light gets in. It is from this quagmire, in muck of these darkest hours that the lotus blossoms. The seed is already within us, our natural inclination towards individuation, healing, and growth. It is our birthright to create our own story, and it is alive in the wellspring of our soul from the very moment we are conceived. All it needs is the light of awareness, willingness to do it differently than our ancestors, and inquiry — *how is this situation inviting me to learn and grow?*

The skills and exercises I have shared in this book form the backbone of my daily practice of getting fierce and breaking the cycle of generational trauma by doing things differently. Placing clear and non-negotiable boundaries around what I am willing to take in and put out has not only given me my own life back, but it has given my daughter her mother back, too. I now have more capacity to pause when I notice a trigger, more willingness to rest when I am tired, more clarity to discern when to engage, and more wisdom to know when to erect a boundary. These practices are precious and non-negotiable because the alternative is so much worse.

My daughter knows now that my meditation time every morning is not something I am willing to compromise, and she knows that I do it because it is the best way to keep the rage monster from leaping out of the closet. I am fiercer than ever in my commitment to keeping myself regulated, rested, and ready for whatever comes at us next. I am so grateful to finally be present to life unfolding and to have these resources in my toolkit for facing life's challenges. Life continues to be unpredictable and uncertain for my daughter and me, but these skills and our commitment to our boundaries are the lifeboat that can keep us afloat on stormy seas, no matter what obstacles life places in our path.

One Day at a Time

She was ten when her dad left and moved across the country, finally leaving us in peace. In the month leading up to his long, confusing goodbye, all I could say with honesty when people asked me how I was doing was that we were "taking things one day at a time."

Even now, one day at a time is all I can manage while still fiercely guarding my wellbeing. If I look too far ahead of that, all of the possibilities and questions swirl together into a clobbering headache, the sinking black hole of despair, and the rising panic of anxiety. I'll admit that I sometimes think about drinking or smoking a joint, just for an evening without awareness of all the suffering in the world. But sobriety is a boundary I will not compromise, as a radical act of compassion for myself and my family, and because I have ended the generation cycle of alcoholism and abuse in my family by saying "no" to dishonoring myself once and for all.

One thing I know for sure, the muck of sober grief, when I am willing to be with it, is much easier to swim through than the concrete sludge of intoxicated, addicted, resisting, seesawing, unhealthy-coping grief.

The waves of pain still come, but without numbing and tuning out, they wash over me and keep moving, rather than pulling me under and holding me there. I don't need wine, weed, or men who treat me like their emotional dumping grounds anymore, because I have learned how to make myself feel better by staying true to my heart, and honoring my body.

I have replaced self-abuse with free-flowing tears, green smoothies, hugs, boardgames, hikes, dinners with friends, horses, and snuggling up on the couch and watching silly television shows that make me laugh out loud. Every night when I go to bed sober, even if I am heavy with emotion and exhausted from surfing urges all day, I congratulate myself. Because tomorrow morning, I will wake up clear-headed and with integrity, prepared to act in the best interest of my daughter and stand my ground in defense of my own wellbeing, for the sake of all the generations yet to come.

Of course, sometimes I wish I could go back in time to those early days of her life that felt challenging for me then, but were so full of possibility for her, when her eyes sparkled with easy joy and effervescence. She is old enough to feel the emptiness of her father's sudden departure from her life. She is wise enough to let him go, but that doesn't make it hurt any less. I can only keep stroking her hair and whispering that everything is going to be okay. And that I'm here, and I'm not going anywhere.

All I have is this moment in time, and the wisdom I've gained along the way. And right now, I am grateful for how her father taught me to get fierce in my boundaries, to furiously defend my convictions, and to guard my bodymind like a precious gem. We can choose to "grow through what we go through," and now that my daughter is halfway grown, I finally know that my job as her mother is to let her find her own way to the surface. I am here for her at the end of the day, with gentle caresses, and bowls of ice cream. But I cannot smile for her. And I cannot unbreak her heart.

I am grateful that I can teach her how to move her anger through her body, how to throw rocks in the creek and scream her pain into the sky, instead of shoving it down inside her. I can teach her that her needs matter, and she does not have to let herself be pressured into compromising herself, just to make someone like her.

Reader, thank you for giving me a reason to write this book. I promise you this. I will not let my daughter wallow in despair. I will teach her to hold her shoulders high with dignity and self-respect. I will show her that she is worth loving, and that she is worth staying for. I will continue to shine brightly in my commitment to radical compassion and sobriety, so that one day the light may start to glimmer in her eyes again.

With grief, fresh starts are everything. So, even though my heart feels heavy a lot of the time, and people who ask how we're doing don't really want to hear all about it, I will keep taking it one day at a time. I have stopped watering weeds and started tending the garden more carefully, because I know that this too shall pass and that we can love ourselves into a brighter tomorrow.

They say the lotus flower blossoms from the mud, and that if there is no mud, there is no lotus. Well, I have dropped lotus seeds everywhere and I *know* that they will blossom because there is plenty of muck for them to root into. Even if I can't see them yet, I *know* there will be flowers because this morning, after heaving herself from bed and trying to keep it together after she spilled milk and cereal all over her favorite jeans, she put on clean clothes, brushed her teeth, did her hair, stepped outside into the sunlight, and then she smiled.

"It's going to be such a beautiful day," she said, brightly, tilting her face towards the sky. "I'm so glad it is finally spring."

To her father, we will continue to take your leaving and your absence one day at a time, and one of these days we *will* get over you. Each time the sun rises we will move on, just a little more. So don't you dare get out there and realize you have made a mistake and try to come crawling back. It's too late for that now. The damage is done. Don't you dare break her heart over and over again. Don't you dare drag us through the mud any longer without giving us space to blossom. We are willing to set you free, you must do the same for us.

I still feel anger about your choices, but I hope you find the healing that you are searching for. Thank you for leaving us in the springtime, so that we can wake up each day to the sound of birds, watch the flowers bloom, and feel the warm sunlight on our cheeks when we step outside.

Boundaries allow you to place a container of care around your sadness, so that you can also give yourself moments to experience pleasure and joy. My sober grief is also fiercely-boundaried grief. It is a radical act of self-care, and a way of saying to the world, "No. I will not go down with this sinking ship. I will wear my lifejacket, and I will commit to being a strong swimmer and not letting myself drown."

To anyone who needs to hear this right now, you do not have to let generations of pain, addiction, abuse, and suffering darken your light. Even if your ancestors and past lovers let themselves sink into darkness and despair, it is still your birthright to shine brightly and stand in the sun and allow the renewal of a new morning to open your heart. It's okay to take it one day at a time.

May all of you here reading these words find space for your own healing, time for rest, and a relationship with yourself that is a refuge. May you know that you are worthy of care and attention. May you be peaceful. May you be safe. May you be willing to light up the darkness with love.

Acknowledgements

Many thanks to my wise and knowledgeable teachers and mentors: Elena Brower, Alan Brown, Patricia Rockman, Susan Woods, Khalila Gillett, Jessica Morey, David Treleaven, Oren Jay Sofer, Janet Curry, Alice Drum, and Reynold Feldman. Thank you for your willingness to teach me, humble me, and for putting up with my many questions and eccentricities.

A world of gratitude to my many friends and family members who offered their life experience and inspired me with their strength and wisdom, or read drafts of this work along the way and helped me finalize the cover artwork: Amy Jo Arndt, Cassie Morningstar, Lyndsay Rose, Kaylea Worm, Tanner Bryce Jones, Judith Oakland, Aneka Van Hansen, Debra Garcia, Steve Magnusson, Amber Diskin, Alicia Witt Thompson, Carmen Sample, Cerise Chamberlain, Thomas Cleary, Deanna Elliot, Mark Moffa, Colleen Schaffner, Roxi Vigil, and Lillian Worm.

I offer the deepest bow of gratitude to my parents, Robert and Barbara Garner, for their unending support of my creative and free-spirited ways, to my ex-husband for teaching me so many valuable life lessons and opening my eyes to generations of abuse, and to my dear daughter, for bearing witness to my healing and giving me purpose, passion, and unconditional love.

Finally, to all my readers and listeners, thank you for your willingness to embark upon this journey, and for not allowing the world to darken your light.

About the Author

Cynthia Garner holds Doctorate in Bodymind Health (DBH) from the Parkmore Institute and an MFA in writing creative nonfiction from Goucher College. She is also a certified meditation teacher, somatic psychotherapist, former classroom teacher, adoptee, and single mom. Her passion is helping trauma survivors find refuge in the present moment, reclaim their power, and come home to their authentic selves. She teaches therapeutic courses online and works with educational leadership and survivors of domestic violence, offering practical coping skills, secular mindfulness, and in-the-moment interventions for managing reactivity and breaking the patterns of generational, systemic, and relational trauma.

She studied counseling at Regis University and is trained in group psychoeducation through the UCSD Medical School, the Centre for Mindfulness Studies, Inward Bound, Mindful Schools, and the Hakomi Institute. She is also a Fulbright Scholar and the author of the memoir *Out of Grace: An Extraordinary Journey through Guatemala's Haunted Highlands*. She attended undergrad at Franklin and Marshall College, where she majored in anthropology and worked as the managing editor of *The College Reporter*.

Cynthia lives in Colorado with her daughter and two dogs, and when she isn't writing or teaching, she enjoys traveling, camping, painting, hiking, horseback riding, songwriting, and playing bluegrass music.

End Notes

---

[1] *The Fist Experiment:* Used with permission from David Treleaven, who adopted it from Staci K. Haines' teachings on trauma, somatics, and social justice, illuminating how to navigate challenges, contractions, and difficulties. Haines, S. K. (2019). *The politics of trauma: Somatics, healing, and social justice.* North Atlantic Books.

[2] *Many terminal medical conditions and diagnoses are stress related:* Mate. Gabor. *When the Body Says No. Caring for Yourself While Caring for Others.* March 6, 2013. Retrieved from https://youtu.be/c6IL8WVyMMs?si=smrUNHmjCd2BThiA.

[3] *Positive moods ripple outward more easily than negative ones.* Cerretani, Jessica. *Harvard Medicine Magazine.* "The Contagion of Happiness." Summer 2011.

[4] *I realized getting through this...:* Halifax, Joan. (2018). *Standing at the Edge: Finding Freedom Where Fear and Courage Meet.* Flatiron Books, New York. p 54-55.

[5] *What have we got on the spacecraft that's good?:* Grazer, B. (1995). *Apollo 13.* United States; Universal City Studios, Inc.

[6] *Catastrophizing:* Kabat Zinn, Jon, Ph.D. (1990). *Full Catastrophe Living: Using the Wisdom of Your Body and Mind to Face Stress, Pain, and Illness.* Bantam Books Trade Paperback, New York.

[7] *Appreciative Inquiry Framework:* Cooperrider, D. L., Whitney, D. K., & Stavros, J. M. (2008). *"Appreciative Inquiry Handbook: For Leaders of Change, Second Edition."*

[8] *The body stores undischarged traumatic energy:* Kolk, Bessel Van Der, M.D. (2015). The Body Keeps the Score. Penguin Books, New York.

[9] *Siegel proposes that everyone has various intensities of emotional experience that we can comfortably experience, process, and integrate:* Siegel, D.J. (1996) *The Developing Mind.* Guilford Press, New York.

[10] *Grant me the serenity to accept the things I cannot change:* Serenity Prayer. Retrieved from https://www.steppingstonecenter.com/addiction-blog/serenity-prayer

[11] Brewer, Judson, M.D. (2018). *The Craving Mind: From Cigarettes to Smartphones to Love.* Yale University Press.

[12] *Arriving at your destination with every step:* Hạnh, T. N. (2022b). *Zen and the Art of Saving the Planet.* HarperOne, an imprint of Harper Collins Publishers, New York.

[13] *Epigenetic research on transgenerational transmission:* Švorcová J. (2023). Transgenerational Epigenetic Inheritance of Traumatic Experience in Mammals. *Genes, 14*(1), 120. https://doi.org/10.3390/genes14010120.

[14] *We develop "schemas" or beliefs about ourselves:* Bowlby, J. (1969). *Attachment and Loss.* Hogarth Press.

[15] *It has a network of 40,000 neurons that function autonomously, like a small brain:* Meda, Karuna. *The Heart's Little Brain.* Thomas Jefferson University. Retrieved on April 19, 2022 from https://research.jefferson.edu/2022-magazine/the-hearts-little-brain.html.

[16] *This phenomenon is known as backdraft:* Neff, Kristin, Ph.D. and Germer, Christopher, Ph.D. (2018) *The Mindful Self-Compassion Workbook.* Guilford Press, New York.

[17] *Infatuated with Columbine:* "Sol Pais died from gunshot wound, autopsy shows." https://www.denverpost.com/2019/08/21/sol-pais-death-suicide-coroner/

[18] *Emotions move through experience like waves lasting about 90 seconds:* Stone, A. M. (2020, November 12). *90 Seconds to Emotional Resilience.* And Robinson, Bryan E. Ph.D. (April 26, 2020). *The 90-Second Rule that Builds Self-Control.* Psychology Today. https://www.psychologytoday.com/ca/blog/the-right-mindset/202004/the-90-second-rule-builds-self-control.

[19] *Our relationship to time has everything to do with how we experience it:* Hendricks, Gay. *The Big Leap.* May 4, 2010. Harper One, New York.

[20] *No act of kindness, no matter how small, is ever wasted:* Quote by Aesop. Retrieved on March 23, 2024 from https://www.randomactsofkindness.org/kindness-quotes/127-no-act-of-kindness-no.

[21] *Warning signs of emotional abuse:* Retrieved from the National Domestic Violence Hotline: www.thehotline.org.

Made in the USA
Columbia, SC
03 May 2024

34784570R00162